David Mountfield

Two Hundred Years Ago

an account of the ejection of the Puritans from the Church of England, and the efforts made to restore them, with a sketch of their rise. Second Edition

David Mountfield

Two Hundred Years Ago
an account of the ejection of the Puritans from the Church of England, and the efforts made to restore them, with a sketch of their rise. Second Edition

ISBN/EAN: 9783337260361

Printed in Europe, USA, Canada, Australia, Japan

Cover: Foto ©Lupo / pixelio.de

More available books at **www.hansebooks.com**

TWO HUNDRED YEARS AGO.

AN ACCOUNT OF

THE EJECTION OF THE PURITANS

FROM THE

CHURCH OF ENGLAND,

AND THE EFFORTS MADE TO RESTORE THEM, WITH A SKETCH OF THEIR RISE.

BY

THE REV. D. MOUNTFIELD, M.A.,

Incumbent of Oxon, Salop.

SECOND EDITION.

LONDON:
KENT & CO., 52, PATERNOSTER ROW.
SHREWSBURY: J. O. SANDFORD, HIGH STREET.
1862.

TO THE

REV. JAMES HILDYARD, B.D.,

RECTOR OF INGOLDSBY,

IN ACKNOWLEDGMENT OF HIS GREAT AND UNWEARYING SERVICES

IN PROMOTING A RELAXATION OF THE

ACT OF UNIFORMITY AND REVISION OF THE LITURGY,

THESE PAGES

ARE DEDICATED BY HIS SINCERE FRIEND,

THE AUTHOR.

CONTENTS.

CHAPTER I.

RISE OF THE PURITANS.—SEVERITIES OF ELIZABETH AND WHITGIFT.—LAUD'S POLICY.—THE REBELLION.—PRESBYTERIANS AND INDEPENDENTS. .. 9

CHAPTER II.

THE RESTORATION.—THE PRESBYTERIANS CAJOLED.—THE HEALING DECLARATION.—SAVOY CONFERENCE.—ACT OF UNIFORMITY. ... 35

CHAPTER III.

BLACK BARTHOLOMEW'S DAY.—THE 2000 CONFESSORS, BAXTER, HOWE, PHILIP HENRY, GOUGE.—SHELDON, MORLEY, GUNNING.—THE MODERATE CLERGY, SANDERSON, PEARSON, JEREMY TAYLOR. 69

CHAPTER IV.

RISE OF THE LIBERAL OR LATITUDINARIAN PARTY.—SOUTHAMPTON, HALE, WILKINS, BOYLE, TILLOTSON, STILLINGFLEET.—THE CLARENDON CODE.—ATTEMPTS TO RESTORE THE PRESBYTERIANS.—THE LIBERAL CLERGY AND THE HIGH-FLYERS.—DR. SAMUEL PARKER. 101

CHAPTER V.

JAMES II. ENDEAVOURS TO INTRODUCE POPERY.—CHURCHMEN AND DISSENTERS COALESCE.—SANCROFT'S SCHEME FOR REVISING THE PRAYER BOOK AND RESTORING DISSENTERS.—THE REVOLUTION.—LORD NOTTINGHAM'S COMPREHENSION BILL.—FACTIOUS CONDUCT OF THE HIGH CHURCH CLERGY.—THE LIBERAL CLERGY PROMOTED.—THE LAST ATTEMPT TO RESTORE DISSENTERS DEFEATED BY CONVOCATION.—SACHEVERELL.—CONCLUSION. 124

If it be evinced that one heaven shall hold men of several opinions, if the unity of faith be not destroyed by that which men call differing religions, and if an unity of charity be the duty of us all, even towards persons that are not persuaded of every proposition we believe, then I would fain know to what purpose are all those stirs and great noises in Christendom.—JEREMY TAYLOR.

What charter hath Christ given the church, to bind men up to more than Himself hath done? Or to exclude those from her society, who may be admitted into heaven? Will Christ ever thank men at the great day for keeping such out from communion with his church, to whom he will vouchsafe not only crowns of glory, but it may be *aureolæ* too, if there be any such things there?—STILLINGFLEET.

The prudence and piety of [the blessed Apostles St. Paul and St. John] those unerring guides of the church, themselves under the certain guidance of the Spirit of truth, directed them to bring the things wherein they would have Christians unite, within as narrow a compass as possible, neither multiplying articles of faith nor rites of worship. These two principles . . . . are both sufficient and necessary, the apt and only means to heal and save us; such as would effect our cure, and without which nothing will.—HOWE.

TWO HUNDRED YEARS AGO.

CHAPTER I.

RISE OF THE PURITANS.—SEVERITIES OF ELIZABETH AND WHITGIFT.—LAUD'S POLICY.—THE REBELLION.—PRESBYTERIANS AND INDEPENDENTS.

WHEN Hooper, on presenting himself to Cranmer and Ridley, for consecration to the bishopric of Gloucester, refused to wear the vestments prescribed to be worn by bishops, he struck the first note of that controversy, which agitated the Church until the ejection of the Puritans at the Restoration of Charles II.* Hooper, like many of the Reformers, regarded the Mass as idolatry, and consequently the vestments which had been worn by the Romish clergy, as idolatrous, and badges of Antichrist; even Cranmer, Latimer, and Ridley, in their last days, spoke of them with contempt.†

When Mary came to the throne, many of the Reformers fled to the Continent, where they probably imbibed from the Swiss Protestants, that dislike of some of the features of the Anglican Church, which they displayed on their return at the accession of Elizabeth. They were much disappointed at the sluggish manner in which that great Queen carried on the Reformation; especially did they dislike the vestments, the

---

* Heylyn calls Hooper the first Nonconformist in England. See also Neal, vol. i. p. 60.
† Sampson told Cecil that he had at his ordination objected to the apparel, but Cranmer and Ridley ordained him nevertheless. Neal, vol. i. pp. 65, 170. Athenæ Oxon. Milton's Reformation in England, vol. i. p. 50.

B

use of which the Queen was unwilling to abolish. Even Jewel, a moderate prelate, speaks of them as "theatrical dresses," "relics of the Amorites;" Grindal, Horn, Pilkington, Sandys, Nowell, Parkhurst, Coverdale, were strongly averse to them, and equally with the Puritans desired their disuse.* Nor were these views confined to a few, they prevailed during the early years of Elizabeth very extensively amongst the parochial clergy, and in the Universities.† At Trinity College, Cambridge, and also at St. John's College, the fellows and students to the number of three hundred, cast off their surplices.‡ At Oxford, there were only three men who could preach, and they were all Puritans.§ Eminent preachers in London inveighed against surplices, rochets, tippets, and caps;** and so widely had these precise or puritanical feelings spread, that a paper presented to Convocation proposing to abolish the use of organs, the observance of saints' days, the signing of the cross in baptism, &c., was rejected by a majority of only one.††

Elizabeth was altogether averse to the nakedness or simplicity to which so many of the Reformers were desirous of reducing the service of the Church; but whilst she wisely refused to yield to their wishes, she unfortunately manifested no tenderness towards those who entertained scruples about the vestments or ceremonies. But the harsh measures to which Parker, the Archbishop of Canterbury, had recourse, instead of producing the desired uniformity, irritated the Puritans,

---

* Zurich Letters, pp. 23, 40, 52, 55, 64, 66, 100, 142, 149, 177. Baxter, part i. p. 32. Neal, vol. i. pp. 170, 173.
† Zurich Letters, p. 168.
‡ Life of Whitgift, by Sir G. Paule, in Wordsworth's Ecc. Biog. vol. iii. p. 561.
§ Athenæ Oxon, vol. i. pp. 374, 550. Neal, vol. i. p. 157.
** Life of Whitgift, p. 560, note 2.
†† Strype, vol. i. pp. 499-506.

and increased their popularity. Parker was succeeded in the Primacy by Grindal, a man of different views. He had shewn himself unwilling to deal rigorously with the Puritans; and soon fell under the Queen's displeasure for his spirited resistance to her commands, requiring him to diminish the number of preachers, and suppress certain religious meetings among the clergy, known as prophesyings. By the Puritans he has been held in reverence as their friend; and in the next century we find the High Church party stigmatising their opponents as Grindalizers.* On the death of Grindal, Whitgift—an upright man, free from covetousness, and on the whole from sycophancy—became Archbishop of Canterbury; he thoroughly entered into the Queen's views, and for nearly twenty years waged war with the obnoxious Puritans.† He endeavoured with indomitable courage, and by innumerable acts of oppression, to carry out the vain design of binding the free spirit of the English nation to a rigid uniformity in public worship. Armed with the tremendous powers of the High Commission Court, he harrassed the puritanical clergy; they were fined, and imprisoned; hundreds of them were suspended and many deprived of their livings: at one time, it was said, a third of the whole beneficed clergy were under suspension for refusing to comply with the habits and ceremonies of the Church.

The sagacious ministers of the Queen were alarmed at Whitgift's violence; Lord Burleigh remonstrated, hinted to him that he resembled a Spanish inquisitor trapping his prey;

---

* Milton calls Grindal "the best of the Reformers, who lost favour for favouring the ministers." Reformation of England. vol. i. p. 10. Collier's Ecc. History, vol. vi. pp. 555, 557. 571, 630.

† Collier, vol. vii. pp. 1, 7.   Grainger's Biog. Hist. vol. i. p. 205.

and the clerk of the Council told him plainly that he would by such proceedings overthrow the Church.*

The policy pursued by Elizabeth towards the Puritans proved an entire failure. At the end of her long reign we find that the Puritans were more numerous, their influence had spread, and their aversion was no longer confined to the ceremonies, but extended to the whole government of the Church. Exasperated by harsh treatment, a violent party had grown up amongst them who demanded the overthrow of the hierarchy, and blackened the characters of the prelates by scurrilous pamphlets. The severities of forty years had failed; mildness and charity might have proved more successful.†

The great Protestant Queen was succeeded by a contemptible Scotch pedant. Whitgift was uneasy about the "Scotch mist," as he called James; the Puritans were full of "brags," for the new King was thought to be a Presbyterian. James had spoken in rather strong terms of the English bishops and the Prayer Book. The latter he had called "an evil said mass in English;" the former he had classed with Papistical prelates.‡

The Puritans presented petitions to the King on his way to London; one was signed by eight hundred ministers, out of twenty-five counties. Their requests were on the whole

---

*Aylmer, Bishop of London, was a far worse man than Whitgift, who was a severe but upright prelate. Macaulay speaks, I think, very much too severely of Whitgift. Collier, vol. vii. pp. 9, 10, 12. Neal, vol. i. p. 423, note. Hallam, vol. i. pp. 200-203.

† Neal says there were about fifteen hundred Puritan ministers in the Church at the close of Elizabeth's reign. Perhaps about one-third of them were in favour of Presbyterianism. But they grew cool on this subject, and most would have been satisfied with moderate Episcopacy. Neal, vol. i. pp. 423, 507; vol. ii. preface, pp. 40 note, 442. Hallam, vol. i. p. 226.

‡ Whitgift's Life, by Sir G. Paule, vol. iii. pp. 616, 617. Neal, vol. ii. pp. 2, 3, 5. Collier, vol. vii. p. 275.

moderate, and most of them might have been granted with advantage to Church and State. The King was not unwilling to display his theological learning, and promised the Puritans that there should be a conference between them and the bishops. The conference took place at Hampton Court, (1603) and lasted three days; four ministers appeared for the Puritans, one of whom, Dr. John Reynolds, was the most learned man in England.* Never did the bishops debase themselves so much, as upon this occasion; towards the Puritans they behaved with insolence, towards the King with offensive servility. They flattered the poor conceited monarch; told him that he was a British Solomon, that never since Christ's time had there been a King like him, and that undoubtedly he spoke by the special assistance of God's Spirit. James dismissed the Puritans with a coarse speech, telling them in his slobbering Scotch fashion, that if they did not conform, he would "harrie them out of the land, or else do worse, only hang them, that's all." No concessions were made to win the Puritans, and thus this happy opportunity of healing the Church's wounds was cast away.†

So ended the famous Hampton Court conference; so will end every conference in which Whitgifts and Bancrofts have the sway. It is idle to say that concession would have been of no avail, that some of the Puritans' requests were trifling, others unreasonable. The answer is short; concession was not tried, reasonable requests were not granted, things indifferent were still forced on tender consciences, the most flagrant abuses in the Church still flourished. The severities which had slackened under Whitgift, for in his latter days he

---

* Athenæ Oxon. Hallam's Literature of Europe, vol. i. p. 119.
† Secret Hist. of the Court and Reign of Charles II., vol. i. Introduction, p. 23, note. Hallam, vol. i p. 297.

became more moderate, and allowed many learned Puritans liberty, so long as they did not openly disturb the Church,* were resumed with terrible vigour by his successor Bancroft,† whose little mind was intoxicated by the most extravagant schemes of ecclesiastical aggrandizement.‡

This fiery and ambitious prelate, unrestrained by the wise ministers who had surrounded Elizabeth, or by James, "who was wallowing like a swine in the mire of his lust," cruelly oppressed the Puritans; hundreds fled from his fury to the deserts of America, until, like his disciple Laud, he interfered to stop the depopulation of the kingdom.

The temperate counsels of such sagacious statesmen as Burleigh and Walsingham, were scorned by the rulers of the Church. They heeded not the warning voice of the great Bacon, who whilst he censured the prejudices, the extravagances and violences of the Puritans, at the same time plainly condemned the persecuting spirit of the prelates, their resistance to reforms and every improvement, their contempt for foreign Protestants, their bad example.§

The severities of Bancroft failed, as had those of Parker and Whitgift. The syren Uniformity whose charms have proved so fatal to church-rulers, was not yet won; and when our British Solomon, an habitual drunkard, liar, and swearer,

---

* Bishop Rudd states that there were divers hundreds so favoured. See his speech in convocation, May 23rd, 1603. Whitgift's Life, pp. 592, 597. Neal, vol. ii. preface, and pp. 28-31.

† "Compared with his successor Bancroft, Whitgift was a valuable prelate." Neal, vol. ii. p. 25.

‡ Bancroft's attempts to prevent the courts of Westminster Hall interfering with the Spiritual Courts, seem to have attracted the attention of Father Paul. That honest Churchman says in one of his letters—"I fear for the English; I hold in suspicion that great power of the bishops, though in subjection to the King. I seem to see the horse saddled in England, and think that before long, the old rider will mount." See Sir Michael Foster's Examination of the Scheme of Church Power.

§ Hallam, vol. i. pp. 327, 395, 396.

died, the Puritans were the most powerful party in the country.*

It was in this reign that a very important change took place in the Church, which had a remarkable effect on the Puritan controversy. During Elizabeth's time the dispute had been concerning the ceremonies and government of the Church; in doctrines both prelates and Puritans were agreed;† all held Augustinian views, and all agreed in interpreting the Articles of the Anglican Church in an Augustinian or Calvinistic sense.‡

But a new school of divines began to appear, and were soon in high favour at court: they were at first known as Arminians, then as Laudians, and a little before the Revolution as High Churchmen. Arminius, from whom they took their name, was professor of divinity at Leyden, where he died broken-hearted by the slanders and persecutions of the Calvinists, whose system he had opposed.*

In England the old-fashioned divines who held what are popularly called Calvinistic opinions, displayed towards the Arminians an intolerant spirit. The pulpits resounded with

---

* Charles I. believed "there was not a wiser man since Solomon" than his father. Clarendon's State Papers, vol. ii. p. 274. Mrs. Hutchinson's Memoirs, pp. 58, 60, 66. Neal, vol. ii. pp. 40, 41, 58,·84. Hallam, vol. i. pp. 227, 298, 394. Clarendon's Hist. vol. i. p. 157. Marsden's Early Puritans, p. 380.

† Bishop Pilkington writing to Gualter (1573) says—"The doctrine alone they [the Puritans] leave untouched; as to everything else they are clamorous for its removal." Zurich Letters.

‡ See Rogers's Preface to his Treatise on the Thirty-nine Articles, written in 1607, and his explanation particularly of the 17th Article.

* The writings of Arminius and his eminent disciple, Episcopius, and probably the increasing study of the Greek fathers, mainly contributed to the decline of Augustin's authority. Bayle's Hist. Dictionary, Articles Arminius, Episcopius, and Vorstius.

angry denunciations of the new heretics, as they were called; and the old controversies about ceremonies and bishops almost ceased.* But the new heretics increased; the most learned divine of the Anglican Church adopted Arminianism; and the High Church party, notwithstanding the taunts of foes, that they sign Predestinarian articles, claim to be the orthodox portion of the Church.† The Puritans suspected that the spread of the Arminians was owing to Court influence, probably not altogether without reason, for they quickly filled the high places of the Church. "What," said a country gentlemen to Morley, afterwards Bishop of Winchester, "do the Arminians hold?" "They hold," said Morley, "the best bishoprics and deaneries in England."‡

The star of Augustin was on the wane. In England and elsewhere, divines began to "bid John Calvin good night;" the institutes of Calvin, hitherto used in the Universities, lost their authority; and before the end of the seventeenth century, the works of Episcopius had taken their place.§

* Clarendon's Hist., vol. i. pp. 156, 159, 163, 164. Sir Philip Warwick's Memoirs, p. 90. Neal, vol. ii. p. 442; vol. iii. p. 27. Potter's Letter to Vicars, in Wordsworth's Ecc. Biog., vol. ii. pp. 438, 439; and vol. iii. p. 283. Hume's History, vol. vii. p. 272. Mrs. Hutchinson's Memoirs, pp. 47, 48, 58. Rushworth, Part I. p. 744. Speeches of Rouse, Pym, and Sir R. Phillips, in the House of Commons, 1628.

† Baxter drily observes, "the doctrinal part of the articles, the Presbyterians generally would subscribe to, but I see not how the reverend brethren on the other side can." Baxter, part ii. p. 214.
So Lord Shaftesbury, in 1675, casts the 39 articles into the teeth of the bishops. "He was extremely in the dark, to find the doctrine of Predestination in the 17th and 18th articles, to be owned by so few great doctors in the Church." Letter from a person of quality, 1675.

‡ Clarendon's Life, vol. i. p. 50. Remonstrance of the House of Commons, 1628.

§ " His works have been very much liked in England, by the Churchmen." Bayle on Episcopius. Hallam's Literature of Europe, vol. iii. pp. 84,-89; vol. iv. pp. 146-148.

There was another important point on which the new school differed from the Reformers. They held that none but bishops could under any circumstances ordain ministers in the Christian Church, and that consequently those who had been ordained in the Scotch and foreign Churches, which had no bishops, were mere laymen.* The chief promoter, though not the originator of these views, was Laud, who before he became Archbishop of Canterbury, exercised a baleful influence in the Church and State. The rapid spread of these new opinions, especially the hateful alliance between the Laudian party and the Crown, against the liberties of the people, alarmed the nation, and immensely strengthened the Puritans. The House of Commons voted that whosoever countenanced Popery or Arminianism, which was supposed to lead to it, should be accounted a public enemy. But the Neiles, Lauds, Mainwarings, and Sibthorpes, encouraged the arbitrary designs of the Court, and continued to drive the nation into the ranks of the Puritans. When Neile and Andrewes, Bishops of Durham and Winchester, were in attendance on James I., the King asked them, "Cannot I take my subjects' money when I want it, without all this formality in Parliament?" Neile readily replied, "God forbid, Sir, but you should; you are the breath of our nostrils!" The King then turned to Andrewes, "Well, my Lord, what say you?" "Sir," he said, "I have no skill to judge of Parliamentary cases." The King answered, "No put off, my Lord; answer me presently!" "Then, Sir," replied

---

* This growing contempt for foreign Protestants was marked and censured by Bacon. The Zurich Letters are the best proofs of the affectionate feelings of the Reformers for the foreign Protestants, whose doctrines they considered to be identical with their own. Zurich Letters, pp. 100, 131, 135, 169. Collier, vol. viii. pp. 166-172. Neal, vol. i. p. 387, and preface to vol. ii. Baxter, part ii. pp. 149, 206. Hallam, vol. i. pp. 395-397.

Andrewes, "I think it lawful for you to take my brother Neile's money, for he offers it."*

The name Puritan had been hitherto applied to one who was opposed to bishops or some ceremonies of the Church. But the Laudian party began to fix it on all who held the old fashioned Calvinistic opinions, or opposed their innovations and arbitrary proceedings in Church or State. If a man refused to dance round the village May-pole on Sundays, or discountenanced the Sunday sports, which chiefly from political motives Laud encouraged, or read the Bible in his family, or prayed at home, or fasted, or went to a neighbouring parish to hear a sermon, or reproved swearers and drunkards, or stood up for the laws of his country and liberties of Parliament, he was railed at as a Puritan.†

Laud now ruled in Church and State without a rival. Seldom had there sat in the chair of Augustin so powerful a prelate.‡ A splendid vision floated before the Primate's mind; the successor of Becket dreamt that the mitre might again confront the crown, the crozier wave over its vassals as well as the sceptre; the high offices of the realm be in the hands of the clergy; canon law supreme; Westminster Hall humbled; Puritans extirpated. Gorgeous ceremonies were revived; churches restored and exquisitely beautified with great zeal,

* Waller's Life, p. vi. (1727).

† Even Sanderson complains of being esteemed a Puritan; and still more strange, according to Barnabas Oley, Nicholas Ferrar was sometimes called a Puritan. "The Arminians," says Shirland, a member of the House of Commons, "have involved all good true-hearted Englishmen and Christians under the name of Puritans." Parl. History, vol. ii. p. 444. Parliament's Remonstrance. December 15th, 1642. Sir B. Rudyard's speeches, Oley's Life of George Herbert, vol. i. p. 107. Mrs. Hutchinson's Memoirs, p. 22. Baxter, part i. pp. 2, 3, 31, 32, 86. Clarendon's Hist., vol. iii. p. 292.

‡ Clarendon's Hist., vol. i. pp. 159, 162, 264, 277; vol. iii. p. 364. Collier, vol. viii. pp. 35, 42.

but no prudence ; communion tables were removed to the east end of the church, railed round, and called altars ; priests and people were to bow to them as they entered and left the church ; rich copes, costly altar-clothes, crucifixes, images, pictures, and credence-tables were introduced. The Laudian clergy performed the service in a strange way, "dopping, ducking, and bowing, as though all made of joints ;" they dressed in a peculiar style ; their priests' cloaks, enforced by the Pope at Lambeth, under pain of ecclesiastical censure, were ridiculed by the people,

> "With a Cardinal's cap, broad as a cart-wheel,
> With a long coat and cassock down to his heel,
> See a new Churchman of the times,
> O, the times ! the times, new Churchman !"

To repress Puritanism, irreligion was set up; to fast was more dangerous than to get drunk, to pray than to swear. Sunday sports were encouraged; the Puritans were struck with horror when they beheld the bishops in the "shamefullest and ungodliest way, pushing forward men to gaming, jigging, wassailing, and mixed dancing on the day which God's law and man's reason hath consecrated." The nation was scandalized by the gorgeous plays and pastorals performed on Sunday afternoons at Whitehall, when also persecution business was transacted by Laud. Sermons full of raillery on Puritans, and almost blasphemous adulation to the King, were preached and cried up by the Court.*

All these proceedings were regarded as certain proofs of a design to restore Popery, and produced great discontent ; yet most of them were innocent, and some of them highly creditable

---

* See the extracts from Wren's, Sibthorp's, and Mainwaring's sermons, given by Mr. Perry in his History of the Church, vol. i. pp. 358, 362, 366. Baxter, part i. pp. 11, 33.   Milton's Reformation, vol. i. pp. 40, 41.

to Laud, for many churches were in a shamefully ruinous state, the services probably slovenly performed, and certainly the communion tables indecently used. Taken alone, they were not sufficient to justify the popular impression; but it is an indisputable fact that the Laudian party made decided advances towards the Church of Rome, which the Homilies of the Anglican Church speak of as idolatrous, a foul, old, withered harlot.* Auricular confession, penance, and absolution, were recommended—to pray for the souls of the dead was lawful—the Pope was no longer Antichrist, the man of sin, the son of perdition, but the chief of bishops, to whom it pertained to summon councils—monastic vows were defended—students at the Universities were recommended to study the fathers and ancient councils, instead of Protestant divines. Laud publicly declared that in the disposal of benefices, he should prefer single before married priests. Not Protestants only but Roman Catholics also believed that this portion of the clergy were bent on restoring Popery.† The Earl of Devonshire's

---

* The following ludicrous instance of the ceremoniousness which prevailed under Laud, is related in the Nonconformists' Memorial.

A clergyman entering a church, went up to the chancel to bow to the altar, upon which a boy was sitting. He seeing the priest make a low bow thinks that it is a mark of respect to him, and bows in return; three times is the bow repeated by the priest and returned by the lad, who is mightily astonished at such civility.

See the proceedings of the Lords' Committee, March 12th, 1641. A paper in the Harleian Miscellany on the causes of the Civil War.

Clarendon's History, vol. i. pp. 136, 168, 169, 172, 348, 496; vol. ii. p. 29. Warwick's Memoirs, p. 81. Warburton's Notes on Clarendon. Welwood's Memoirs. Canons of 1640 (Canon vii.) in Sparrow's Collection. Collier, vol. viii. pp. 93 94, 180. Marsden's Early Puritans, p. 355. Homily against peril of Idolatry.

† See the Instructions from the Pope to his Nuncio in England, in Clarendon's State Papers, vol. ii. p. 44. May's Hist. of the Parliament, Book i. pp. 19, 22, 24. Welwood's Memoirs. Collier, vol. viii. pp. 120-122, 171, 172. Proceedings of Lords' Committee, March 12, 1641. Hallam, vol. ii. p. 63.

daughter having become a Romanist, was asked by Laud the reason. "'Tis chiefly," she said, "because I hate to travel in a crowd." Laud desired her to explain her meaning. She replied—" I perceive your Grace and many others are making haste to Rome, and therefore, in order to prevent my being crowded, I have gone before you."*

As Laud and his party became more friendly to Rome, they became more scornful towards the foreign Protestant churches. The Cranmers and Hoopers, the Jewels and Grindals of the Reformation had taken sweet counsel with the Bucers and Martyrs, the Bullingers and Gualters of the continent; but now the Laudian party accounted all churches which had not bishops as no better than sacriligious laymen. Instructions were given to our ambassadors abroad, no longer to countenance such Puritanical rebels. In France, Lord Scudamore withdrew from the Protestant Church at Charenton, and it was industriously spread abroad that the Anglican Church did not regard foreign Protestants as brethren. This, said Lord Falkland, was an action as impolitic as ungodly. †

Nor was this the only measure by which Laud succeeded in converting the foreign Protestants into enemies. He and his creatures, particularly Wren and Neile, passionately and furiously proceeded against the French, Dutch, and Walloon congregations settled in London, Canterbury, Norwich, and

* Hume, vol. iv. p. 408.
† Clarendon says in a letter to Secretary Nicholas—"The English church taught not such coyness towards the Reformed churches; you and I, if we were in Germany might, and I think ought to communicate with the church of Luther with all charity and alacrity." From this and other papers, it appears that Clarendon recognised the foreign Protestant churches. Clarendon's State Papers, vol. ii. pp. 308, 317, 337, 401-404. Clarendon's Hist. vol. iii. pp. 364-368. Collier, vol. viii. pp. 50, 56-58, 91, 100, 101. Milton's Reformation, vol. i. p. 38. Falkland's Speech on Bishops. For Charles I.'s opinion on the Foreign Churches, see Clarendon's State Papers, vol. ii. pp. 433, 434.

elsewhere ; treacherously breaking through the charters, by which they had been protected.*

Whilst Laud was thus coquetting with Rome, disparaging and alienating from us Protestant princes and commonwealths, he was irritating the nobility by advancing the clergy to the highest offices of the realm. He thought that temporal honours and splendour would beget a reverence for his order ; they were made justices of the peace ; they swarmed about the court ; Juxon, Bishop of London, was created Lord High Treasurer of England ; it was rumoured that Wren, Bishop of Norwich, was to be made Secretary of State ; and Bancroft, Bishop of Oxford, Chancellor of the Exchequer. The gentlemen of England hated the little, low-bred, red-faced man, who swayed and carried all things before him in the Privy Council and High Court,† and as the prelates rode to Westminster, people merrily called them "The Church Triumphant."‡ Meanwhile Laud was displaying his fierce, cruel character, by a furious persecution of the Puritans. Great numbers of them forsook their dear home, their friends and comforts, and fled for refuge to the vast howling wildernesses of America, until Laud in an evil hour for himself and his royal master procured an order to prohibit their migration.§ "They were persecuted in the Bishop's Courts, fined, whipt, pilloried, imprisoned ;

---

* Clarendon's Hist., vol. iii. pp. 364, 365.

† See Lord Digby's Speech, Nov. 9th, 1640—"Does not every Parliament man's heart rise to see the prelate's usurping," &c.; also Mrs. Hutchinson's Memoirs.

‡ Laud got also, says Clarendon, the Archbishop of St. Andrews made Chancellor of Scotland, a thing not known since the Reformation ; Clarendon's Hist. vol. i. pp. 152, 154, 163, vol. iv. p. 437 ; May's Hist. Book I. pp. 19, 22, 24 ; Milton's Reformation, vol. i. p. 43 ; Laud's Diary, March 6th, 1635.

§ Religion stands on tiptoe in our land,
Ready to pass to the American strand.
GEORGE HERBERT.
Cromwell's Speech, Sept. 12th, 1654. Milton's Reformation, vol. i. pp. 37, 39.

they suffered barbarous mutilations, ear-croppings, nose slittings, and brandings; they could enjoy no rest, so that death was better than life itself."* But oppression was producing its bitter fruits. A vindictive spirit was spreading among the people; the disgusting mutilations inflicted on Prynne, Bastwick, and Burton, three noted Puritans, in the palace-yard at Westminster, inflamed the multitudes who witnessed them; seditious libels were dispersed about London, menacing Laud with destruction; the mob full of fury, collected around Lambeth, breaking the windows, and threatening to pull the Archbishop out of his palace. The rebellion was drawing near.†

In the year 1640, that memorable year in which England, after a long period of oppression, rose up to regain her liberties, Laud resolved to strike a blow, and rid the church of the Puritan clergy, or silence their clamour for reforms.

To bishops, such as the early church possessed, the Puritans did not generally object, but they thought that the prelates of the Anglican Church did not resemble the Clements and Polycarps of ancient times, and it was well known that they looked with little favour on Archbishops, Deans, Archdeacons, Chan-

---

* "In their High Commission and Star Chamber Courts, they lent themselves to much sanguinary and oppressive work, ear-cropping, nose-slitting, ruinous fining, and long imprisonment." Warburton's Memoirs of Prince Rupert. Mrs. Hutchinson's Memoirs, pp. 64, 66. Clarendon's Hist. vol. i. pp. 161-163, 170. For the manner in which the Calvinistic clergy were vexed by the Laudian bishops, see Bishop Hall's Observations in Wordsworth's Ecc. Biog. vol. iv. pp. 288-290; also Wren's Articles, which are a choice specimen of malice and tyranny.

† Clarendon admits that when Laud became Primate the nation was little inclined to the Papist, and less to the Puritan. Collier is possessed with Clarendon's idea, that if the persecution had been a little sharper, it would have been successful. "Had not," he says, "the rebellion come on, Laud would, in all likelihood, either have converted or crushed the Puritan sect." Clarendon's Hist. vol. i. pp. 162, 163. Collier, vol. viii. p. 174. Welwood's Memoirs, p. 36. Sir Philip Warwick's Memoirs, p. 79. Warburton's Notes on Clarendon. Neal, vol. ii. pp. 277, 287. Baxter, part i. pp. 13, 14.

cellors, &c.* An oath, therefore, was invented by the Convocation, which met to frame canons, to be taken by all the clergymen, schoolmasters, &c., that they approved the doctrine and government of the Church, and would never "consent to alter the government by Bishops, Deans, Archdeacons, &c., as it stands now established, and as by right it ought to stand." Those who refused to take this astounding declaration, were to be cast out of their livings. This audacious invasion of the liberty and property of the subject, which was not without precedent, is the last attempt made by the clergy to impose an oath on Englishmen without the consent of Parliament, and was the finishing stroke of a policy which aimed at reducing men to an intolerable slavery.† The canons passed by Convocation excited great dissatisfaction. Some said they made the king an absolute monarch,‡ others objected to the offensive ceremony of bowing to the altar, which they recommended ;§ but all the Puritans were opposed to the "etcœtera oath," as it was called. Many considered that Convocation had no power to impose an oath on Englishmen; others said that there were some things in the church which they wished to see reformed, and therefore could not swear that they would never consent to alterations. The opposition increased; moderate

* Baxter presses on Bishop Brownrigg "the practice of the Church till Cyprian's time, as a probable notice to us of what was the apostolical government; if you cast off the example of Cyprian's times, why use the argument of antiquity for Episcopacy?" Although antiquity favours Baxter, it is doubtful whether the Puritan form of Church government would have been favourable to religious liberty—Baxter, part i. p. 178.

† See the canons of 1640, in Sparrow's Collection; they will satisfy most men that Laud and his party regarded the king as independent of Parliament. The most important question raised by these canons, is the power of Convocation to impose an oath, without consent of Parliament. Laud's policy has, and always will have, many admirers amongst the clergy; Convocation is steadily advancing its old pretensions, and writers such as Collier, Walker, Carwithen, and others, claim for it the power of imposing oaths. Collier, viii. pp. 180, 181.

‡ See the first of the canons of 1640. § Canon VII.

Churchmen seeing the rising storm, pressed Laud to pause in his mad career. Sanderson, one of the most learned divines of the Anglican Church, called by Archbishop Usher, "the judicious Sanderson," wrote to Laud, telling him that multitudes of Churchmen, not of the preciser sort alone, but well-affected and regular, would utterly refuse it, and the Church be in danger.* The pious Bishop Hall would not tender it to any of his clergy.† At last, the opposition becoming more alarming, the nobility advised the King to interfere, and he wrote to the stubborn Primate, forbidding it, for the present, to be pressed.‡

One of Laud's early friends had foretold that if he went on as he began, he would one day set the nation on fire. The prophecy was fulfilled; the nation was on fire; the Great Rebellion, as it is called, had commenced.

Parliament met Nov. 3rd, 1640; it was that Long Parliament which began so well, and ended so ill. The great patriots were there; in counsels as yet undivided, animated by one lofty purpose, to deliver their beloved country from the civil and religious tyranny which it had been suffering.§ There

* Nalson's Collection, I. p 497. Baxter, part i. pp. 15, 16. Neal, vol. ii. pp. 336. † See his Observations on his Life, and Letter to a friend, both reprinted in Wordsworth's Ecc. Biog. vol. iv. pp. 289, 293.

‡ An instance of the crushing despotism of Laud is to be found in the Clarendon State Papers, vol. ii. p. 117. The King was at York, whither Dr. Burgess, a Puritanical clergyman, went to present a petition from his brethren, (I suppose against the Canons;) when the Council in London heard of it, they instructed Windebank to write to the King, recommending him to commit Burgess, and any petitioners, close prisoners for their insolency. Windebank's Letter is dated Sept. 18th, 1640. Clarendon's Hist. vol. i. pp. 252, 260.

§ According to Clarendon, all except Lords Say and Brook in the House of Lords, and Nathaniel Fiennes, St. John, and Vane in the Commons, were attached to the Church.

Baxter says, that the members of the Long Parliament living in 1673 profess that they know of but one Presbyterian in the House at the beginning. Baxter, part i. pp. 31, 34; part iii. pp. 41, 149. Clarendon's Hist. vol. i. pp. 240, 322-326, 329, 330, 347 note f, 355-357, 408-410, 536; vol. iii. p. 312. Neal, preface to vol. ii. and p. 444.

were Lord Falkland, John Hampden, Lord Digby, Hollis, Sir B. Rudyard, Grimstone, Selden, "the glory of the English nation," with those other powerful lawyers, whom Laud had arrogantly sought to humble, Pym, Maynard, Coke, Whitelock, Langhorne, Bagshawe, Glynne,* and one Oliver Cromwell, with a "thread-bare coat, and a greasy hat."† These great men condemned with virtuous indignation the insolence and tyrannies of the Laudian prelates. Lord Falkland, whilst eloquently defending the venerable order of bishops, rebuked those prelates who had so grievously abused their sacred function. They had, he said, brought superstition and scandal into the church,—had slackened the union between us and foreign Protestants, an impolitic as well as an ungodly act,—had sheltered Papists, and ruined Protestants for scruples,—had cared more for conformity to some ceremonies than to Christianity,—had suppressed preachers, and like the dog in the fable, would neither preach themselves nor let others preach,—had cried up the sacredness of tithes and priests,—had brought in as much of Popery, and destroyed as much of the Gospel as they could, without bringing themselves in danger of the Law,—had been betrayers of our rights and liberties,—and, in short, not content with arbitrary power in ecclesiastical matters, had grasped at an equal power in temporals. Lord Digby, also a Royalist, was more severe on the Laudian prelates. He said, no one was more aware than himself of heavy grievances in the church, no one more anxious to clip the wings of the prelates, by which they had mounted to such insolence; none had been able to escape

* The lawyers were hostile to the Laudian bishops, "who had shewed contempt for the supreme courts of law, and thereby made the lawyers very undevoted to them." Clarendon's Hist. vol. i. p. 496., vol. ii. p. 29. Sir Philip Warwick's Memoirs, p. 81.

† South's Sermon at Westminster, Feb. 22nd, 1684.

their vengeance: was there a man of tender conscience, him they loaded with unnecessary impositions; was there a man of a legal conscience, him they nettled with innovations, and fresh introductions to Popery; was there a man of an humble spirit, him they trampled to dirt in their pride; was there a man of a proud spirit, him they have bereft of reason, with indignation at their superlative insolence; was there a man faithfully attached to the rights of the Crown, how has he been galled by their new oath; was there a man that durst mutter against their insolencies, he may inquire for his lugs; they have brandished not only the *spiritual* sword of St. Peter, but the *material* one too, and cut off ears; let us reform these things, and reduce bishops to their primitive standard, but let us not extirpate them.*

Parliament proceeded in a most judicious manner to redress the grievances of the nation. They swept away those engines of arbitrary power, the Star Chamber, and High Commission Courts; they pronounced the late oath and canons illegal, and to preserve the liberties of the people from the encroachments of ecclesiastics, declared that the clergy had no power to make laws for the church without the consent of Parliament;† they impeached Laud of High Treason, and released his victims from the dungeons in which they were rotting. Prynne, Burton, and Bastwick returned from their distant prisons; they entered London in a sort of triumph; great multitudes of people accompanied them, with rosemary and bays in their hats, crying in the greatness of their joy,

---

* Nalson's Collection, vol. ii. pp. 211, 276. Rushworth, part iii. vol. i. Neal, vol. ii. pp. 391-405.

† The Commons came to these resolutions concerning the canons, nullo contradicente; the Lords concurred. In their Remonstrance of the State of the Kingdom, (1642), the Commons say, "The canons and the power of canon-making are blasted by the vote of both houses." See Parl. Hist. vol. ii. pp. 826, 863. Paxter, part i. p. 27.

"Welcome home, welcome home, God bless you, God be thanked for your return." The hated Laudian clergy dare scarcely officiate in their churches; as they walked through the streets, they were taunted as Popish priests, Cæsar's friends.*

The misguided King now saw his error. He was willing, he said, that some law might be made to give liberty to tender consciences, in matters indifferent;† he promoted moderate divines to bishoprics,‡ and instructions were given for a revision of the Prayer Book. Laud, quailing at the storm, directed Sanderson, with two assistants, to make some safe alterations in the Prayer Book, and remove or leave indifferent those pitiful ceremonies which for eighty years the rulers of Church and State had been forcing on the Puritans. At the end of five months Sanderson's reforms were completed. § But concessions came too late; the nation was drifting into civil war. For eighty years had the Puritans been harassed and oppressed; James had driven them from his presence with an insolent threat; Charles had sought to root them out as noxious weeds; and the result of all these oppressions and severities and cruelties was that England was Puritan.

The struggle between the King and Parliament now commences; the nation resounds with arms. Rupert and his troop of horse fly about the country; insolent, debauched soldiers,— "dammes" as the people called them from their common oath,— plunder and abuse noted Puritan ministers as rebels; the Parliamentary troops, equally ill-treat the Royalist clergy, as

---

* Athenæ Oxon, Prynne. Neal, vol. ii. p. 372. Fox's Hist. pp. 8-10. Baxter, part i. pp. 16, 26.
† See the Declaration to the People, 1641. Clarendon's Hist. vol. ii. p. 142.
‡ Prideaux, Winniff, Brownrigg, Henry King, and Westfield, of the Puritanical school, were made bishops; and Usher was appointed to Carlisle. Clarendon's Hist. vol. ii. p. 25. Collier, vol. viii. pp. 198, 240, 241. Athenæ Oxon, Articles King and Prideaux. Neal, vol. ii. p. 480.
§ Sanderson's Life by Walton, in Wordsworth's Ecc. Biog. vol. iv. pp. 420, 421.

malignants.* The Parliament finding itself hard pressed by the King, seeks assistance; the Scotch Presbyterians are called in "to the help of the Lord against the mighty;" they march into England with their "solemn league and covenant," stuck upon their pikes; the reforms proposed by the moderate bishops and divines, Usher, Williams, Morton, Hall, Sanderson, Prideaux, are abandoned, and revolution commences; the Anglican Church is overthrown, and through the interest of the Scotch, Presbyterianism becomes supreme; Laud is murdered; and the clergy driven from their livings.† Some of them probably were no loss to their parishes, being drunkards, swearers, ignorant as well as ungodly; but others were good men, holy and learned, who had done no man wrong, a Hammond, a Jeremy Taylor, a Prideaux, a Hall, a Nicholas Ferrar; these men were treated with remorseless bigotry, insulted, robbed, beggared, imprisoned,‡— sixteen hundred in all, according to some, two thousand four hundred, according to others; the use of the Prayer Book was prohibited, and in fact the whole frame-work of the Anglican church destroyed.§ But the true authors of its sufferings were

* Mrs. Hutchinson's Memoirs, pp. 94, 95. Anthony à Wood's Life, p. vii. Baxter, part i. pp. 44, 45. Neal, vol. iii. p. 24. Warburton's Memoirs of Rupert, &c., vol. i. p. 390.

† The settling of Presbyterianism, says Kennet, was by the fear and love of the Scotch army; when they left, rigid Presbyterianism died. "Overdoing," says Baxter, "is the ordinary way of undoing. Interest forced or led Parliament to call in the Scots, and Presbytery came in with them." Baxter, part i. pp. 27, 48; part ii. p. 369; part iii. p. 149. Sanderson's Life in Wordsworth's Ecc. Biog. vol. iv. p. 419.

‡ "Have they not by imprisonments or threats, muzzled the mouths of the most grave and learned preachers of London?" Rupert's Declaration, given in Warburton's Memoirs, vol. ii. p. 122. Bishop Hall's Hard Measure. Lives of Hammond, Sanderson, &c. Pepys's Life, vol. i. p. 257.

§ The sufferings of the Puritans through the reigns of Elizabeth, James I. and Charles I. were greater than those of Churchmen during the rebellion. Bramhall and Heylyn state that there were many more ejected by the Presbyterians, than had been by the bishops. But it must be remembered that some were ejected for notorious immorality, and cannot be considered martyrs; nor were the jails crowded by Churchmen during the rebellion, as they had been by Puritans, nor do I know of one instance of a Churchman being the Bancrofts, Neiles, Lauds, Mainwarings, Sibthorpes, Wrens, Montagues, Heylyns, with their slavish sermons and speeches, their obstinate resistance to reforms, their scorn for other Protestant churches, their arrogance and tyranny, their branding-irons and barbarities, cowing the free spirit of our forefathers, presumptuously checking the ancient laws, labouring to exempt priests from the magistrate, slighting the majesty of Parliament, and seeking to thrust the laity under a despotic monarch, that they might more easily become their own slaves. It was these things which drove the nobles, gentry, yeomen, and traders of England into rebellion and Puritanism.*

branded, or having his ears cut off, or his nose slit. We cannot know with any accuracy the number of clergymen ejected by the Parliament; they were deprived at different times and for different causes; some for refusing the "solemn league and covenant," a solemn iniquity; some for refusing the engagement; some for vice and ignorance; and some for what was called "malignancy," that is attachment to their Church and King. Baxter says, that as far as he knew, six to one at least, if not more of the sequestered clergy were proved insufficient or scandalous or both; most of them were gross drunkards, &c.; a few civil men who assisted in the wars against Parliament, and set up bowing to altars and such like innovations were ejected. Fuller is less favourable, for whilst he admits that many scandalous ministers were deservedly punished, and "much corruption let out, so at the same time the veins of the English Church were also emptied of much good blood." Neal seems to think that the number of ejected clergy was about 1600; and taking Nalson's list as a basis for calculation, that is the number; other lists give 1726 and 1800. Walker repeats Gauden's statement that 7000 were ejected, but cannot support it, for he gives two lists, one of the ejected clergy, the other of the livings from which they were ejected; the former contains, I think, about 1400 names, the latter about 2700. A fifth of the income was allowed for the support of the ejected clergymen's families. Collier, vol. viii. pp. 262, 263, 375. Baxter, part i. pp. 74, 95; part iii. p. 98. Clarendon's State Papers, vol. ii. p. 363. Neal, vol. iii. pp. 124-127. Hallam, vol. ii. pp. 164-166.

* Sir Matthew Hale says, I am confident that had the bishops laid aside some ceremonies that were of no great moment in themselves and were too strictly imposed, the State, civil and ecclesiastical, would never have been convulsed, nor episcopacy ever been brought low. Charles II. said the bishops had ruined his father. Very remarkable is the conversation related by Hyde, between Sir Edmund Verney, the King's standard-bearer, and himself. "I will deal freely with you," said Sir Edmund, "I have no reverence for the bishops, for whom this quarrel subsists." "Yet," says Clarendon, " his affection for the Church has never been disputed." Clarendon's Life, vol. i. pp. 134-136.   Baxter, part iii. p. 41.   Milton's Reformation, vol. i. pp. 43-44.

The Puritans or Presbyterians, as they were henceforth called, shewed themselves apt imitators of the prelates. The episcopal arts begin to bud afresh, exclaims the indignant Milton, they who of late were little better than silenced from preaching, seek to silence us from reading except what they please. The gentlemen of Cheshire complained to Parliament, that instead of twenty-six bishops, there was now a pope in every parish, for every minister exercises purely papal jurisdiction.

"And every hamlet's governed,
By 's holiness, the Church's head." *

The rigid Presbyterians clamoured for the suppression of sects and schisms, declaimed against what they called the damnable doctrines of toleration and liberty of conscience; and during their brief supremacy, laboured to establish a spiritual tyranny as intolerable as that of Laud. They denounced in most violent language, the notion that all men should enjoy liberty of conscience. Toleration, they said, was a root of gall and bitterness, —a door to libertinism and profaneness,—foul poison. A leading Presbyterian minister writes thus: "Toleration will spoil any church and government. If Presbyterial government be settled, and a toleration be given in this land, that will mar all." Again, "I humbly beseech the Parliament seriously to consider the depths of Satan in this design of a toleration; how this is now the last plot and design,—it is his masterpiece for England." He calls toleration *an innocent-looking devil*, and concludes with these words: " Farewell, the Lord keep thee and all thine from all evil: and especially from *noon-day devils*, which walk about in this place, and in these times; from the errors of Anabaptists, &c.; toleration of sects and schisms, under pretence of liberty of conscience."† Another writer says: " To

* Hudibras, part i. canto iii.   Areopagitica, vol. i. pp. 314, 315.   Remonstrance from Cheshire gentlemen.
† Antapologia, by Thomas Edwards, minister of the Gospel, 1644.

let men serve God according to the persuasion of their own consciences, is to cast out one devil that seven worse may enter." In 1647, the London Presbyterian ministers put forth a "testimony against the errors, heresies, and blasphemies of these times, *and the toleration of them.*" The last error against which they bear witness is the "error of toleration," and they complain of this as a great grievance, "that men should have liberty to worship God in that way and manner, as shall appear to them most agreeable to the word of God."*

The bigotry of the Presbyterians provoked the army, which was chiefly composed of Independents. Those grim soldiers had not been fighting at Edge Hill, Newbury, Marston Moor, and Naseby for ship money, or other merely civil immunities, but for that which is above all liberties, "liberty to know, to utter, and to argue freely according to conscience."† The army, or its master, Cromwell, expelled the Presbyterians from Parliament, beheaded the King, and established a Republic. The Independents claim the high honour of being the earliest to assert and practice the great principles of religious toleration; to them or to the Baptists the honour seems to belong.‡ But though they were much in advance of the Presbyterians, their views were still very imperfect, as is shewn, not only by their conduct in New England, where they were dominant, and where they

* This testimony was approved by 360 Presbyterian ministers. In 1648, the Presbyterians persuaded Parliament to pass a law against heretics, by which all who maintain certain opinions, which are specified, were *to be put to death.* This awful law was never enforced, although the Presbyterians eagerly pressed Cromwell to take away the life of a harmless man, John Biddle, who held Arian views.—See the life of Biddle, in the Biog. Brit. vol. ii. p. 306, note N.   Neal, vol. iii. pp. 274, 280-289, 360, 458. Firmin's Life, p. 7.   Mrs. Hutchinson's Memoirs, pp. 199, 210, 232, 234, 242, 250, 264, 269, 284, 363.   See also Selden's and Whitelocke's speeches on the Presbyterians, in Whitelocke.

† Areopagitica, vol. i. 325.

‡ In 1614 a treatise in favour of toleration appeared, called "Religious Peace, by Leonard Busher." In 1615 the Anabaptists boldly claimed the right of every man to judge for himself.   Neal, vol. iii. pp. 516, 530.

persecuted, but also at home. Even Dr. Owen, "the patriarch of Independency,"* who wrote so well on the subject of toleration, could sentence two Quaker women to be whipped out of Oxford ;† and neither he nor his brethren would tolerate Papists, Arians, Quakers, and Socinians.‡

Presbyterianism, as it flourished in Scotland,§ happily never took root in England ; it was a stranger here. So that, though the Puritans were henceforth "called by the vulgar, Presbyterians, and they submitted to the Scotch system, yet they were for moderate episcopacy."|| The Presbyte-

* Milton was unwilling to tolerate Popery and open superstition. Areopagitica, vol. i. p, 328. So in his treatise on civil power in Ecclesiastical Causes, he says, but with evident hesitation, he will not plead for Popery and Idolatry. † Neal, vol. iv. p. 282.
‡ One of Cromwell's Parliaments appointed some Presbyterian and Independent divines to determine what were the fundamentals of Christianity. This was, as Baxter says, a ticklish business, and as it throws light on the progress of liberal views, I have thought it desirable to notice it in this note. Baxter at once proposed that the Apostles' Creed, Lord's Prayer, and Ten Commandments should be offered to Parliament, as containing all things necessary to salvation. Dr. Owen and Dr. Cheynell objected, saying Papists and Socinians will subscribe all this. Baxter replied, so much the better, and so much the fitter it is to be the matter of our concord. He was, however, over-ruled, and twenty articles were forwarded to Parliament, the effect of which would have been to exclude from toleration Papists, Arians, Socinians, Quakers, and many others. Baxter, part ii. pp. 197-205. Neal, vol. iv. pp. 97-101.
§ Scotch Presbyterianism was a tyranny, compared with which that of the Anglican prelates was mild. The laird of Drum being threatened with excommunication by the persecuting Presbytery said to them,—While you hold the reins, there is no indulgence for neither minister nor laird, no condition or sex; you complain of the pomp and grandeur and titles of the bishops, but you have exceeded them ; your little finger has been heavier than the weight of the episcopal body; the Kirk is hardened against compassion, its strongest arguments are the pike and musket. Collier, vol. viii. pp. 370-373. See also the treaty of the Scotch with the King, Dec. 26th, 1647,. in Clarendon's History, vol. v. p. 533.
|| "In the county of Worcester," Baxter says, "he knew of but one Presbyterian. Almost all that were called Presbyterians, were before the wars Conformists, they esteemed the moderate bishops, Davenant, Hall, Usher, Morton. I know not of two Non-Conformists in a county ; but they disliked and resisted the Book of Sports, &c. There was but one Presbyterian known in all the Parliament. The truth is, Presbytery was not, at the beginning of the wars, known in England, except among a few studious scholars, nor well by them." Baxter, part i. pp. 33, 34, 97, 146 ; part ii. pp. 41, 146. Clarendon's History, vol. v. p. 338.

rian or Puritan clergy were a respectable body of men; they were strict in their lives, zealous pastors, and able preachers. But they were narrow-minded and intolerant, very apt to think that no one could get to heaven except in one way, which was *their* way, and struggled against Cromwell's liberal design of establishing liberty of conscience.* Speaking accurately, there was until the Restoration, no Established Church; the benefices were held by Episcopalians, Presbyterians, Independents, and Baptists.†

---

* Cromwell was a man of large and liberal views. Undoubtedly he treated the Anglican Church with great severity; but churchmen were his active political enemies, continually engaged in conspiracies and assassination-plots. Yet Gunning and other clergymen officiated as openly as Dissenters did after the revolution. Guizot's History of Oliver Cromwell, vol. ii. pp. 110, 111, 154, 155. Baxter, part i. pp. 46, 48, 50, 51, 53; part ii. p. 214.

† Warburton says, "The Presbyterian was to all intents and purposes the Established religion during the Commonwealth." With this Hallam disagrees; for if benefices were held by Independents and Baptists, and the Presbyterians could not exercise coercive discipline, how can Warburton's assertion be correct? Hallam ii. p. 200, note c. Baptists held benefices, for they were excepted by the Convention Parliament, when they secured other Incumbents. See 12 Car. ii. cap. 19.

CHAPTER II.

THE RESTORATION.—THE PRESBYTERIANS CAJOLED.—THE HEALING DECLARATION.—SAVOY CONFERENCE.—ACT OF UNIFORMITY.

THE death of Oliver Cromwell was expected to be followed by tumults and confusions; but Richard succeeded his father without a murmur of opposition. All men wondered to see things so quiet; the Royalists were amazed.* The young exiled King and his courtiers were sadly disappointed at the unexpectedly tranquil state of England. Though in deep poverty, Charles II. kept up the form of a Court during his exile. He had his Lord Chancellor, Chancellor of the Exchequer, Privy Counsellors, and Secretaries of State; though not one of His Majesty's servants had a pistole in his pocket. To Mr. Secretary Nicholas, who had been complaining of want of money, Sir Edward Hyde, afterwards Earl of Clarendon, writes, "I want shoes and shirts, and the Marquis of Ormond is in no better condition."† Hyde was the King's chief adviser; he had distingushed himself in the beginning of the Long Parliament as a patriot; but like the Falklands and Southamptons was offended by the excesses of the Puritans. Exile and sharp poverty had extinguished the remains of his patriotism; and now his aim was to restore Church and State to the condition in which they were before the meeting of the Long Parliament. Charles II. was entirely guided by this able,

* Baxter, part i. p. 100.
† Clarendon's State Papers, vol. iii. pp. 174, 229.

faithful, and on the whole virtuous minister, to whom he willingly left the affairs of the kingdom, that he might attend to others of a different kind, for he had already abandoned himself to Lucy Barlows, Catherine Pegs, and Elizabeth Killigrews. It is hard to say what Charles's religious views were, further than that he thought God would make no man miserable for taking a little pleasure. The Scotch pressed him to abide by the covenant which he had taken; the Roman Catholics endeavoured to make him a proselyte; Hyde and Ormond laboured to preserve him steady to the Anglican Church. The careless King listened to all, and scandalized all by the number and publicity of his amours.

England soon found how great a man it had lost in Oliver Cromwell; the tranquillity of his son's first days of power was soon broken; affairs began to fall into utter anarchy, "all was confusion, no government, no magistrate, the Parliament turned out by the army, and the soldiers quarrelling among themselves."* The army dissolved the Parliament, restored the contemptible Rump amidst the scorn of the people, pulled down Richard Cromwell, dissolved the Rump, set up a Council of State, again restored the Rump, in short disgusted the nation, and prepared the way for the triumphant restoration of the King.† A general rising was projected by the Presbyterians, who with very few exceptions were in favour of a limited monarchy,‡ and Cavaliers; but the latter were dispirited by repeated failures, and left the former to fight alone. They were quickly

---

* Evelyn's Memoirs, vol. i. p. 306.
† Collier, vol. viii. p. 382. Mrs. Hutchinson's Memoirs, pp. 336-360.
‡ "The Presbyterians," writes Bordeaux to Mazarin, "who are now predominant, do not wish the King of England to return unconditionally." There were extremely few Republicans among the Presbyterians; their political views were more just and sound than their ecclesiastical views. The Independents were generally Republicans. See Mrs. Hutchinson's Memoirs, pp. 296-299, 303, 305, 322. Clarendon's History, vol. vii. p. 376. Guizot's History of the Restoration, vol. ii. p. 351.

suppressed; yet nothing daunted, the Presbyterian ministers persevered in rousing the loyalty of the nation. They did not conceal their aversion to the Republican Government, "prayed very seditiously in their pulpits," and told the people that it was their duty to return to their allegiance. "Leave the game in our hands," said Hollis, one of the Presbyterian leaders, to the Cavaliers, "we alone have any chance."* The Presbyterians were encouraged in their labours by solemn promises from the Cavaliers of love and charity; letters were received from Dr. Morley, then with the King, declaring that all moderation was intended; that any episcopacy how low soever would be accepted; that Archbishop Usher's moderate scheme or Bishop Hall's, was all that was intended; that there should be no persecuting Lord Bishops, no great revenues, no godly able ministers displaced, much less silenced, no unworthy men put in, no thoughts of revenge for anything past, but all should be equal.†

When Monk, upon whom all eyes were now fixed, reached London, the ministers waited on him, urged him to cast aside the reserve which he had maintained, and declare for the King.‡ The zealous labours of the Presbyterians were not in vain. After some vacillation, and much lying, Monk cautiously took measures for restoring to Parliament the Presbyterian members who had been expelled by Oliver Cromwell. The poor old Rump, which had been restored by the Republican party, was sitting; they were in the agonies of despair, suspecting Monk's real intentions, yet unable to resist him. The secluded members returned; once more the Presbyterians were supreme; and the Republic was at an end.§

---

* Mrs. Hutchinson's Memoirs, pp. 333, 346, 362, 363. Clarendon's History, vol. vii. pp. 322, 332, 333, 439-441. Guizot's History of the Restoration, vol. ii. p 15. Baxter, part ii. pp. 207, 214.
† Baxter, part ii. p. 208.
‡ Baxter, part ii. p. 214. Fox's Hist. of James II. p. 19.
§ Guizot's Hist. of the Restoration, vol. ii. pp. 140, 141.

Some of the Presbyterians wished at once to restore the King, under sufficient securities for the laws and liberties of the nation; but the Long Parliament had become odious; the people were impatient for its dissolution; the streets were crammed with multitudes crying out for "A Free Parliament, a Free Parliament." "Pray be quiet," said Monk, "you shall have a Free Parliament." The famous Long Parliament, whose end was as impatiently wished for as its beginning devoutly prayed for, was dissolved, and the writs for a Free Parliament issued.* There were great rejoicings when it was known that a free Parliament was to be called. In the city the bells were ringing; London "looked as if it had been in a flame by the bonfires, which were prodigiously great, at which rumps of beef were roasted." From London to Land's End bonfires were blazing on the hills.† "In Oxford, the bells rang and bonfires were made, and some rumps and tayles of sheep were flung into a bonfire. Dr. John Palmer, a great rumper-warden of All Souls, had a rumpe thrown up from the streets at his windowes."‡

The reaction in favour of the King was now steadily increasing. As the hopes of the Cavaliers rose, they began to threaten revenge. The more cautious Royalists were alarmed at these imprudences, and hastened to disown such uncharitable sentiments. The vigilant Hyde instructed his agents to sharply rebuke these "Ranters."§ He writes to one of his correspondents, probably Barwick:—Some of your divines have been using menaces and threats; the least offence should not be given; they should teach others by their example and doctrine, to make better use of their late sufferings than to

---

* Clarendon's Hist. vol. vii. pp. 418, 419.
† Aubrey's Lives, vol. ii. pp. 453-457.
‡ Anthony Wood's Life, vol. i. p. 40.
§ Clarendon Papers, vol. ii. pp. 713, 716, 722, 727.

retain any bitterness or uncharitableness in their hearts; the King is really troubled at these excesses, and commands that all good and prudent men should endeavour to extinguish jealousies and apprehensions, that Church and State may be happily settled. This letter was circulated amongst the Royalists, by Barwick, who also wrote to his friends, regretting that charity had been forgotten. He reminds them that the want of this great virtue was the original of all their sufferings, that without it the unhappy differences cannot be composed, and concludes by hinting how useful it would be for the nobility and chief gentry in the several counties, "to make some public declaration of their willingness to forget what is past, and lay aside all animosities for the future, and freely acquiesce in what the Parliament shall do, in order to a happy settlement."‡ The Royalist nobility, gentry, and clergy about London, published a declaration in which "they sincerely professed that they reflected on their past sufferings as from the hand of God; and, therefore, did not cherish any violent thoughts or inclinations against any persons whatsoever." They further pray, that when Church and State shall be built up again, "all mention of parties and factions, and all rancour and animosities, may be thrown in and buried like rubbish under the foundation." Similar declarations were published by the Cavaliers in Dorset, Somerset, and other counties.§

Extraordinary pains were taken to allay the rising suspicions of the Presbyterians. Foreign Protestant ministers wrote to Baxter and his friends, assuring them that Charles was an excellent prince, and a sound Protestant. Even Hyde blushed not to propagate falsehoods, and deceive the nation as to the

‡ Somers Tracts.
§ Clarendon Papers, vol. iii. pp. 713, 722, 727, 731, 732.   Clarendon's Hist. vol. vii. pp. 471-473. Sir Phillip Warwick's Memoirs, pp. 464, 465.

real character of the King; he declared him to be the best of Protestants, the best of Englishmen.* Dr. Morley, afterwards Bishop of Winchester, was sent over by Hyde; he had frequent meetings with the city clergy who were Presbyterian, and promised that all former offences and animosities should be forgotten, that there should be henceforth meekness, charity, and moderation. He reported to Hyde the results of his labours:—The moderate Presbyterians were agreeable to bishops, provided they could not act arbitrarily or tyrannically, and also to the Liturgy, with some little alterations, and liberty to use extempore prayers on special occasions; the chief difficulty was concerning ordination; but he had thought of two expedients; the Presbyterians wanted a Conference, but he told them it would be better to refer their differences to a Synod and Free Parliament. He assured them that the King was fully sensible of what they had done in producing the great and happy change in his affairs, that he doubted not but they would do much more for him, and he "was sure they would have no cause to repent of it." We shall see whether Baxter and his friends had "no cause to repent of it." Everything was done "to sweeten the crabbed Presbyterians."* "I hope," writes Barwick to Hyde, "no acts or artifices are omitted to dispose them, for their own sakes, as much as is possible to repair the ruins they have made."‡

Monk was in secret communication with the King; and before the meeting of the new Parliament had admitted Sir

* The Earl of Southampton afterwards expressed resentment at the deception of Clarendon. Evelyn was deceived, as appears by his curious tract in reply to the "News from Brussels"; bitter and bad as this last is, it is nearer the truth than Evelyn's. See both in the Somers Collection. Clarendon Papers, vol. iii. p. 541.

‡ Clarendon Papers, vol. iii. pp. 720, 722, 723, 731, 736, 738, 744. Rapin's Hist. vol. ii. p. 613. Carte's Ormond Letters, vol. ii. p. 337. Marvell's Works, vol. ii. p. 212. Burnet's Hist. of his Own Time, vol. i. p. 150.

John Grenville, the king's agent, to a private interview. Monk, who was a moderate Presbyterian, and had recommended that moderate Presbyterianism should be established,* advised Charles to send him a letter to be presented to Parliament, in which were to be laid down the bases of the king's Restoration. Hyde accordingly composed the royal declaration, sent it to Monk, who ordered Grenville to keep it until the proper moment arrived for its production. This was the celebrated declaration from Breda. We shall see how this royal charter was observed.

The Presbyterians were now resuming possession of power all over the country; they occupied the best livings in London and elsewhere; they possessed the Universities and the chief garrisons, and in the Convention Parliament as it was called,—not being summoned by the king's writ,—they were powerful.† A few days after the meeting of the Convention Parliament, the royal declaration from Breda was read; there was a great shout of joy throughout the House; the two Houses invited the king to return; and the ancient constitution was re-established. The clause concerning religion runs thus: " We do declare a liberty to tender consciences, and that no man shall be disquieted or called in question for difference of opinion in matters of religion, which do not disturb the peace of the kingdom; and that we shall be ready to consent to such an Act of Parliament as upon mature deliberation shall be offered to us, for the full granting that indulgence."

* "Moderate, not rigid, Presbyterian government," he said to the Rump Parliament, "with a sufficient liberty for consciences truly tender, appears at present to be the most indifferent and acceptable way to the Church's settlement." Clarendon's Hist. vol. vii. p. 415.

"The Presbyterians were, in Monk's opinion, the most powerful, and, perhaps, the most national party." Guizot's Hist. vol. ii. p. 15.

† "The Presbyterians are now in possession of the supreme power." Bordeaux to Mazarin. Guizot's Hist. vol. ii. pp. 140, 141. Clarendon's Hist. vol. vii. p. 481.

D

On the 8th of May, the sun rose with unusual splendour; the propitious omen brought tears of joy to the eyes of the loyal; for on that day Charles II. was proclaimed king of England, Scotland, France, and Ireland.* Calamy, Reynolds, Manton, and other leading Presbyterian ministers went over to Holland and waited on the king; they assured him of their loyalty, that they laboured for his restoration, that they were no enemies to moderate Episcopacy, but only desired liberty in some things which they considered unlawful, and hoped that he would not direct his chaplains to use the surplice and read the whole of the Liturgy, lest the people might take offence. The king received them kindly, acknowledged their services, said that he had no intention of imposing hard conditions, and embarrassing their consciences, and that he had referred the settling all differences to the Parliament. But his majesty decidedly rejected their advice as to the surplice and Prayer Book,—he would not be restrained himself, he said, but would enjoy the liberty that he gave to others.† He never denied them a private audience; and so delighted them by a prayer which they overheard him offering up in an adjoining room,—that the Lord would give him an humble, meek, forgiving spirit,—that one of the ministers lifted up his hands to heaven, and blessed God that he had given them a *praying* king. The Presbyterians returned and repeated to their brethren the king's encouraging promises of peace.‡

On the 29th of May, 1660, Charles II. rode into London, "the bells ringing, the ways strewed with flowers, the streets hung with tapestry, the fountains running with wine, trumpets, music, and myriads of people shouting with inexpressible joy."

* Clarendon Papers, vol. iii. pp. 742, 743.
† Clarendon's Hist. vol. vii. pp. 501-503. Collier, vol. viii. pp. 383, 384.
‡ Baxter, part ii. p. 218. Neal, vol. iv. pp. 252-254.

It seemed, as the king merrily said, that it was nobody's fault but his own that he had remained so long abroad when all mankind wished him so heartily at home.* All the island began to grow mad, says Mrs. Hutchinson; some people, it is said, died from excessive joy. Old William Oughtred, the mathematician, was lying on his bed very sick; he heard that the king had returned, and asked his friend, "And are ye sure he is restored? Then give me a glass of sack to drink his majesty's health;" and then he died.† The London ministers attended the king, and presented him with a richly adorned Bible, which he told them should be the rule of his actions; and forthwith commenced his connection with Barbara Palmer. Ten of the leading Presbyterian ministers were placed on the list of the king's chaplains.‡

There was now a glorious opportunity of healing the Puritan dispute, and enlarging the foundations of the National Church. A century had passed since the Reformation; it had been a century of wearying controversy between prelates and Puritans; all that could be said by either party had been said; both had suffered; neither were without faults; and as promises had been given that the past shall be buried, and there shall be henceforth moderation, meekness, and charity; there seems nothing to hinder a speedy and happy settlement of the affairs of the church. But the tide of popular feeling was now setting in strong against Puritanism, and in a few weeks after the Restoration, the once powerful Presbyterians were so unpopular that their ministers could scarce venture into the streets without being insulted. Their windows were broken, their psalm-singing was drowned by the blowing of horns; it became the fashion to revile the snivelling, canting, rebellious

---

* Evelyn's Memoirs, vol. i. p. 310. Clarendon's Life, vol. ii. p. 2.
† Aubrey's Lives. Mrs. Hutchinson's Memoirs, pp. 358-362.
‡ Baxter, part ii. p. 218. Echard's History, p. 771.

Presbyterians, a generation of vipers, unlikely to escape the damnation of hell; the ballad singers sung up and down the streets ribald rhymes on the late times and the actors therein. This violent reaction was noticed with pleasure by the Court, and perhaps suggested the treacherous policy which was henceforth pursued towards the Presbyterians.*

There soon appeared in the Convention-Parliament two parties, the Presbyterian or moderate, and the Court party, who were in favour of what Clarendon calls "the old principles of Church and State."† The moderate party were anxious to effect a settlement of the ecclesiastical affairs of the nation; but the Cavaliers, instructed by Hyde, a master in Parliamentary tactics, perplexed and obstructed them.‡ However, after some opposition from the Cavaliers, an Act was passed for restoring the ejected clergy, and confirming those who possessed benefices, of which there was no other legal claimant. This was a wise measure; by it all the ejected clergy were restored, including those who had been ejected for scandalous offences, whom the Puritans unreasonably thought should not have been restored.§ A bill for settling religion was introduced, and the second reading was fixed for June 30th, 1660; it was postponed to July 2nd, and again to July 6th. It was then read a second time, and referred to a Grand Committee for Religion, which was ordered to meet every Monday. At the first meeting of this Committee there was a long debate; it

---

* Baxter says, that those men are reprovable, who say that nothing but deceit and juggling was from the beginning intended; the prelatic party, until they saw the reaction were glad of the terms of the Declaration of Breda. Baxter, part ii. pp. 287, 376. Mrs. Hutchinson's Memoirs, p. 366. Neal, vol. iv. p. 325.
† Clarendon's Life, vol. ii. pp. 16, 17.
‡ Clarendon's Life, vol. ii. p. 17.
§ Neal speaks of it as a most monstrous thing that scandalous clergy should be restored. Hyde disliked the Act for obvious reasons. See his Speech, Sept. 13th, 1660. Neal. vol. iv. pp. 261, 312. Clarendon Papers, vol. iii. p. 747. Collier, vol. viii. p. 404. Rapin, vol. ii. p. 621.

was proposed to adjourn; this was opposed by others. The speakers waxed warm, for an hour they remained in the dark; candles were then allowed to be brought in; twice were they blown out, but the third time they were preserved, though amidst great disorder. The struggle lasted until ten o'clock, when it was voted, that the king should be desired to select a number of divines, to whom the matter might be referred, and the Committee adjourn till the 23rd of October next.*

It is possible, and it is charitable to think, that Hyde had been sincere in his negociations with the Presbyterians before the Restoration; but it scarcely can be doubted, that now he and his friends had formed the intention of breaking faith with them.† The Presbyterians were uneasy, and pressed the King to interpose and settle the differences in the church. Charles good-humouredly told them that to effect a settlement each party must give up something, that so they might meet in the middle; and it should not be his fault, he said, if they were not brought together. Old Mr. Ash, much reverenced for his simplicity and holiness, burst out into tears of joy, and expressed the gladness which his majesty's words had put into his heart.‡ After much writing and going to and fro, the king, as head of the church, said he would publish a declaration containing the concessions which he thought should be made. On the 25th of October, 1660, the anxiously-expected declaration appeared, it caused great joy to all moderate men, breathing, says Bishop Kennet, "a spirit of truth and wisdom and charity above any one public profession

---

* Journal of the Commons, and Parl. Hist. Clarendon's Life, vol. ii. p. 139.

† Hyde's party had promised to abide by the decision of *this* Parliament. See Dr. Morley's Letter to Hyde, written at the time the elections were being made, April 3rd, 1660, in the Clarendon Papers, p. 722. See also the king's answer to the Presbyterian ministers at Breda, and Clarendon's Life, vol. ii. p. 139.

‡ Baxter, part ii. pp. 231, 234. Pepys's Diary, vol. i. p. 85.

that was ever yet made in matters of religion." Another learned churchman says, that next to the Bible he adores this admirable declaration, which would have established a firm and lasting concord.* The moderate Puritans were delighted; and great was the applause bestowed upon this Healing declaration.† Baxter, who had almost despaired of union, hearing the king's declaration, cried in the streets, stepped into a coffee-house to read it; as he read, he wondered, he says, how came it to pass, but was exceeding glad, for now the terms were such as honest, sober ministers might accept. He went to Lord Chancellor Hyde, heartily thanked him, and rejoiced to see factions and parties swallowed up in union, and contentions turned to brotherly love and concord. But the yearnings of this generous man after Catholic communion were laughed to scorn by men whose consciences were seared, and hearts hardened.‡ Bishoprics were offered to the leading Presbyterians. Baxter refused the bishopric of Hereford, that he might have more influence in inducing all his brethren to comply. Reynolds at once accepted the bishopric of Norwich. Calamy was offered the bishopric of Lichfield. Doctor Manton accepted the living of Covent Garden from the Earl of Bedford, and was offered the deanery of Rochester; Dr. Bates the deanery of Lichfield; Mr. Bowles the deanery of York; they were not without suspicions that some deception was being practiced on them, but were willing to accept these high posts when the Healing declaration became law. The Presbyterian ministers of London drew up an address of thanks, and, with the learned Matthew Poole at their head, waited upon the king, by whom they were most graciously received. "Gentlemen," said Charles, in his usual pleasant way, "I will endeavour to give

---

* Kennet's Hist. vol. iii. p. 246.   Echard's Hist, p. 781.
† Ralph's Hist. vol. i. pp. 19, 20.   Baxter, part ii. pp. 284, 366. Lingard's Hist. vol. xii. p. 27.   ‡ Baxter, part ii. p. 279.

you all satisfaction, and to make you as happy as myself.* The House of Commons waited upon his Majesty, and returned thanks for his gracious declaration. Their Speaker said—He could not express the great joy and thankfulness of the Commons, for his majesty's labour and pains, repairing and making up our breaches and unhappy differences. His Majesty had provided, in his gracious declaration, which had given general satisfaction, strong meat for those able to bear it, and milk for tender babes, dispensing with conformity in some things indifferent. The Commons are unanimous in giving thanks, and have ordered a Bill to be drawn. Your Majesty hath not only Jacob's voice, but Jacob's hands; you have spoken kindly to your people, and you have handled them gently; may you have Jacob's blessing; let your people serve you, and let the nations of the earth bow down before you; those that curse you, let them be cursed, and they that bless you, let them be blessed.‡

In accordance with the order of the House the leader of the moderate church party, the excellent Sir Matthew Hale, whose large heart was rejoicing at the liberal concessions of the king, brought into the Commons a Bill to pass the declaration into law. The disputes which for well-nigh a century had rent the church were about to be healed, and the Puritans of England dwell at peace in the church of their forefathers. But over this bright scene a dark cloud creeps. Hyde, now Earl of Clarendon, and the bishops, dislike the concessions which the king has made; instructions are given to the Court party; Sir Matthew Hale is taken out of the way by being raised to be Chief Baron of the Exchequer, and on the 28th of November, after a long adverse speech from Morrice, one of the Secretaries

---

* Neal, vol. iv. p. 309. Athenæ Oxon., Manton.
‡ Ralph's Hist. vol. i. p. 25.

of State, the Bill embodying Charles's declaration is thrown out on its second reading, by a majority of 26 in a House of 340. It is clear now that Clarendon and his friends were merely amusing the Presbyterians, until it was safe to drop the mask.*

In this declaration the king promised that as the Presbyterians objected to several things in the Prayer Book, it should be reviewed. Accordingly next year (March 25th, 1661) a commission was issued to twelve bishops and twelve Presbyterians, with nine assistant divines on each side. They were to review the book of Common Prayer, to consider all the objections which had been raised against it, and make such reasonable and necessary alterations "as shall be agreed upon to be needful and expedient for the giving satisfaction to tender consciences, and the restoration of peace and unity." The commission was to last four months, and they were to meet at the lodgings of the Bishop of London, in the Savoy; hence this is called the Savoy Conference. On the part of the Presbyterians, Baxter and Calamy were the leaders; on the Episcopal side, Sheldon and Morley. Baxter acted imprudently, he asked for too much; Sheldon acted with gross unfairness, baffled the Presbyterians, and shewed on the first day they met, his determination that the Conference should be a failure. To waste time, for the delay as Bishop Short says, could hardly be accidental, no meeting was appointed until three weeks had been lost. Their first meeting was on

---

* Ralph says, had there been sincerity in this Healing declaration, a general union might then have been obtained, but one of the Secretaries of State, it was presumed, by command opposed it, upon which a negative ensued, and it was heard of no more. Ralph's Hist. vol. i. pp. 20-25. Secret Hist. of Charles II. vol. i. pp. 32, 33, 89. Kennet's Hist. vol. iii. p. 246, note b, and p. 252, note a. Burnet's Hist. of his Own Time, vol. i. pp. 305, 307. Neal, vol. iv. p. 307. Clarendon's Life, vol. 2, p. 143. See the preface to Clarendon's Hist. vol. i. p. 21.

April 15th. The Archbishop of York opened the proceedings by stating that he knew little about the business, and that he should therefore leave it to Sheldon, Bishop of London, who had the king's instructions. The Archbishop never spoke again at any of the meetings; probably he did not fall in with the views of Sheldon and that party, for he was a quiet peaceable man, and supposed to incline to Puritanism.*

Sheldon opened the business by proposing that Baxter and his friends should put down in writing all their objections, as well as the additions and alterations which they desired. To this the Presbyterians objected, and humbly prayed for a friendly conference in order to come to an agreement as to what concessions could be made on each side. But Sheldon and his party would not hear of this; they were resolved not to treat the Presbyterians as equals; they knew that the Ministers who once had so powerfully acted on the people were at their mercy; and the mercies of angry ecclesiastics are cruel. The effect of Sheldon's proposal was what he intended it to be. It divided the Presbyterians; some were for insisting only on a few important matters, believing that if they were gained and a comprehension effected, it would be easy to settle other disputed points; unfortunately this prudent advice was not followed, through the fault of Baxter it is generally supposed. He persuaded his party to put down all their objections, and offer all the alterations which seemed to them desirable, although he acknowledges that he saw the trap laid for them by Sheldon.† In about three weeks they completed their paper of exceptions. It was sent in May 4th. The Bishops were frightened at its length, and Sheldon was enabled to succeed in that which was his design from the beginning,—not to make any concession, any attempt

---

* Kennet's History, vol. iii. p. 253.   Baxter, pp. 305, 363.
† Baxter's defence is that Sheldon commanded them to deliver *all* their exceptions.

to promote union. Nay, he confessed thus much a short time afterwards, for he said to Lord Manchester : "Now we know their minds, we'll make them all knaves if they conform." The commission directed that some additional forms should be drawn up. The Presbyterians assigned this task to Baxter, and again did Baxter shew himself to be wanting in those qualities which were needed in dealing with men, like Sheldon, quick to take advantage of the mistakes and faults of their adversaries. He was guilty of what some call a piece of insolence.* It was certainly a foolish and even presumptuous act; instead of drawing up a few additional forms, he composed in fourteen days an entirely new Prayer Book, which he called "The Reformed Liturgy." This proceeding had, as we might expect, a most mischievous effect. Burnet says, nothing gave the Bishops so great an advantage over Baxter and his party, as their offering a new Liturgy. Whatever Baxter's object was, he shewed a sad want of common sense. As soon as the Reformed Liturgy was received by the Bishops, it was rejected without examination. With the paper of objections, the Presbyterians sent a petition to the Bishops, begging them with great earnestness not to force upon them the ceremonies to which they object, and using a variety of arguments to induce the Bishops to charitably bear with the infirmities of the weak, saying, "Grant us but the freedom which Christ and his Apostles left to the churches; use necessary things as necessary, and unnecessary things as unnecessary." The Presbyterians having delivered their papers, retired, and anxiously awaited the reply of the Bishops. This was the critical time of the Conference; it was now in Sheldon's power to gain the moderate Puritans. And nothing can be plainer than the directions given in the Scriptures for the treatment of weak consciences; but there is no truth which men will not

* Wheatly on the Prayer-Book, p. 30.

dispute, no precept which they will not disregard if it thwarts their interests or passions. When the reply came, instead of being as the ministers were expecting, a list of the concessions which the bishops were willing to make, it proved to be a reply to their exceptions, and did not contain one concession which the opposite party cared for. Papers went backwards and forwards, sharp things were said on both sides; Sheldon was obstinate and unyielding; Baxter by nature hasty and impetuous, indignant at the treachery and ingratitude of the prelates, indulged in threatening, contemptuous, irritating language. Thus matters stood, each party angry and exasperated with the other. Ten days more and the commission expired. The Presbyterians again requested that there might be a friendly conference as the best means of coming to an agreement. This request when made at the first meeting, Sheldon had peremptorily refused, but now he granted it. When they met, the Ministers desired the Bishops to give their opinions on the alterations and additions which had been suggested, declaring what they allowed and what they disallowed. But the Bishops refused to give their opinion on the papers that had been sent. They then asked the Bishops to go over the points in dispute, and declare how much they could abate, and what alterations they could yield to. To this moderate, reasonable request, again did Sheldon and his party give a decided refusal. The baffled ministers again and again urged the words of the king's commission. In the Healing declaration the king had said, "since we find some exceptions made against several things therein, [the Prayer Book,] we will appoint an equal number of learned divines of both persuasions to review the Book of Common Prayer, and to make such alterations as shall be thought most necessary;"*

* 7th clause of the King's declaration.

and the words of the commission were still more explicit, they were to "advise and consult upon and about the several objections and exceptions which shall now be raised against the same, and, if occasion be, to make such reasonable and necessary alterations, corrections, and amendments, as shall be agreed upon to be needful and expedient for the giving satisfaction unto tender consciences, and the restoring and continuance of peace and unity in the churches under his majesty's protection and government." "These words," say the Ministers, "imply that some alterations must be made." The Bishops answer : Yes, *necessary* alterations and such as should be agreed on, but we don't consider them *necessary* until you prove them necessary, and we don't *agree* upon them. The Ministers reply to this unworthy quibble : We are called together to make such alterations as are necessary *to satisfy tender consciences;* we are to consult on the *means,* and if you, the Bishops, will not *agree* upon anything we suggest, the conference is a sham, all our meetings are but trifling and useless. The Bishops stick to their text : Prove your alterations to be *necessary.* After wrangling for some time about this word *necessary,* a disputation was agreed upon, after the manner of the schools. Three on each side were chosen to manage the dispute, but it was chiefly carried on by two men, "the most unfit to heal matters and the fittest to widen them," Baxter and Gunning. There was much logic,—keen, sharp arguing—for these intellectual duellists were well matched in debating powers. Of course no good result could follow from such an absurd proceeding ; and after many interruptions, the debate ended abruptly amidst great confusion. Towards the close of this sham conference, a sensible proposal was made by some important personage, that Baxter and his party should put down those points on which they considered forcing compliance was sinful. They mentioned eight, and *in* *not one of those eight points would the Sheldonian party make any concession.**

As the Hampton Court Conference had ended, so ended the Savoy Conference, so will end every conference in which Sheldons and Morleys have the rule. The promises of charity and moderation made but twelve months before, were violated; the meekness then affected was exchanged for a scornful smile. The times had changed. "Let it be as God will," said Mrs. Hutchinson to one of Clarendon's followers, when pleading for her husband. He, smiling at her, replied, "It is not now as God will, but as we will."†

When the Savoy Conference had come to an end, the Presbyterians again tried the Lord Chancellor, and prayed him to use his power to pass the Healing declaration into law, or advise them in what way they were to proceed. Clarendon promised to present an address from them to the king: accordingly the address was drawn up and presented. In it they give an account of their proceedings, and further express themselves thus: "We must needs believe that when your majesty took our consent to a Liturgy, to be a foundation that would infer our concord, you meant not, that we should have no concord but by consenting to this Liturgy, without any considerable alteration. And when you comforted us with your resolution to draw us together, by yielding on both sides what we could, you meant not that we should be the boat and they the bank that must not stir. And when your majesty commanded us by your letters patent to treat about such alterations as are needful or expedient for giving satisfaction to tender consciences, and the restoring and con-

---

* Marvell's Works, vol. ii. p. 500.   Burnet, vol. i.   Kennet's History, vol. iii.   Baxter, part ii.; part iii. p. 104, and Appendix viii. p. 121.   Secret History of Charles II. vol. i. pp. 149, 349.   Neal, vol. iv. pp. 337-345.   Collier, vol. viii.

† Mrs. Hutchinson's Memoirs, p. 381.   Hallam, vol. ii. 320, 336.

tinuance of peace and unity, we rest assured that it was not your sense, that those tender consciences were to be forced to practice all which they judged unlawful, and not so much as a ceremony abated them; or that our treaty was only to convert either part to the opinion of the others." They conclude by beseeching the king that the Healing declaration might be established, so that piety and peace may flourish.* But all their entreaties were of no avail, their fate was already decided upon, and the House of Commons had commenced that career of vindictive fury, which for ten years they pursued without remorse.

Some important events had been meanwhile occurring, which will explain the indignant, despairing, threatening language which Baxter had been using in the late Conference. The Convention Parliament was dissolved, Dec. 1660. Clarendon had experienced some difficulty in managing it; and as he could not trust it to pass the severe acts which he was meditating against the Presbyterians, his object, as he scarcely conceals, was to amuse them until another Parliament more suited to his purpose could be assembled.† The new Parliament met May 8th, 1661. It lasted eighteen years; and for the first ten years of its existence proved itself the blindest, the most bigoted, intolerant, slavish Parliament, that ever met in this country.‡ It contained only fifty-six of the Presbyterian or moderate party; most of the others were red-hot Cavaliers, many were more violent even than Clarendon. It was elected according to the wishes and by the influence of the Court; in a word, says Rapin, it was composed by Clarendon, prime minister. It is asserted that one hundred of them were in constant pay,

* Baxter, part ii. pp. 367, 368.
† Clarendon's Life, vol. ii. pp. 17, 139, 143.   Secret History, vol. i. pp. 32, 33, 89.
‡ North's Examen, pp. 361, 426.   Lord Campbell's Lives of the Lord Chancellors, vol. iii. p. 205.   Clarendon's Life, vol. ii. pp. 260, 273.

receiving large sums from the exchequer; they were called the Club of Voters, and this Parliament is known as the Pensioned Parliament.*

Clarendon now saw that it was safe to cast off the mask,—the king was seated on the throne of his ancestors,—the church restored to her ancient privileges,—Cromwell's terrible army was disbanded,—the Presbyterians had become unpopular, and above all, a Parliament had assembled eager for revenge. At the opening of the new Parliament, he recommended seditious preachers to be suppressed. A few days after, (May 16th, 1661,) the House of Commons resolved that all members should take the Sacrament according to the rites of the Church of England on pain of expulsion. Before the close of the year, Clarendon's famous "Corporation Act" was passed, expelling all Nonconformists from corporations,—an act contrary to the assurances given by Morley and Clarendon,—contrary to the king's promise that no man was to be molested on account of his religion,—contrary to the plainest principles of justice and religion. There was a strong disposition to renew the Laudian tyrannies, and revive the odious Star Chamber. "Things goe very well on in the Houses of Parliament," writes the Dean of Durham to a friend, "I believe you will hear of a repeal of all acts made in the Long Parliament; and then the Starre Chamber, and High Commission will return of course."† But this divine's pleasant anticipations were not realized; Laud and the branding irons did not return; the noses and ears of Englishmen were henceforth safe. The Puritans, alarmed at the black storm that was gathering over them, flew now to one great man, now to another, and sometimes promises were made

---

* Rapin, vol. ii. p. 625.   Sir Thos. Brown's Works, vol. i. p. 8.   Lord King's Life of Locke, p. 137.   Parl. Hist., vol. iv. p. 178.
† Letter from Sudbury, Dean of Durham, to Dr. Basire, April 11th, 1663.—See Basire's Correspondence.

that the king would interpose, and by an indulgence protect them from persecution. But Clarendon was preparing for his next blow; it shall be effectual, mercy and truth shall be forgotten, malevolence and perfidy shall carry the day.*

With the Pensioned Parliament assembled the Convocation of the Clergy; and such care was taken in keeping out and getting in members, that Sheldon and Morley were able to carry all their plans. Although many of the Presbyterians had been ejected from their livings in consequence of the old incumbents being alive, and others prevented voting, the Presbyterian ministers in London were strong enough to return Calamy and Baxter by three voices; but Sheldon chose two others, so they had no seats in Convocation.† Sheldon and his party had already agreed upon their plans. A worthy clergyman out of Huntingdonshire, one Dr. Allen, who had come up to attend Convocation, earnestly urged Sheldon to reform the Prayer Book, and remove the exceptions of the Presbyterians, Sheldon quietly told him there was no need to trouble himself further about that, as they had resolved upon their measures.‡ During the adjournment of Parliament and Convocation, the Bishops were employed in revising the Prayer Book. They were not all of one mind; some, whom Clarendon says were the most experienced and wise men, were for making no alterations but adhering to the old Prayer Book; a second party were anxious to conciliate; but there was a third party who were resolved to gratify their bad passions by inserting in the Liturgy reflections on the Puritans.§ On Nov. 21st, 1661, the king's letter was

---

* Sir Thomas Brown's Works, vol. i. p. 14.
† Kennet, vol. iii. p. 251, note A.   Baxter, part ii. pp. 333-334. Neal, vol. iv. p. 350.   Barnet, vol. i. p. 316.
‡ Calamy's Life of Baxter, p. 160
§ Clarendon's language is most strange, he lets the truth escape from him in one passage, and in the next endeavours to destroy its effect.—See Clarendon's Life, pp. 278-282.

read in the Upper House, authorising Convocation to make alterations in the Prayer Book, and in one month the whole was finished and subscribed Dec. 20th, 1661, thus confirming the remark made by Sheldon, that matters had been already agreed upon. When the alterations (there were six hundred) appeared, it was found that whilst the public were reckoning on some conciliatory changes, Sheldon and Morley had not only made no concessions but had seized the opportunity to make the Prayer Book more distasteful to the Puritans than before.* The deception which Sheldon and Morley practiced did not escape observation, and was afterwards flung in their faces. Lord Shaftesbury said— under the advantage of a pretence well-known to us all, of making such alterations as might the better unite us, the Liturgy was made the other day, more different from the dissenting Protestants ; and there is scarce one alteration, but widens the breach.† Their mode of dealing with the Apocrypha is the most remarkable specimen of this wicked schismatical spirit. The Presbyterians strongly objected to lessons being read from the Apocryphal books, and had petitioned that lessons from Canonical books should be substituted. This very moderate request was not only rejected, but it was proposed in Convocation that some more of the Apocryphal books should be read, such as the History of "Bel and the Dragon," "Susannah and the Elders," and this proposal was carried. Andrew Marvell tells us, that after a long tug about that matter in Convocation, a jolly doctor came out, his face radiant with joy, and with

---

* This is admitted by those who have no sympathies with the Puritans. Alexander Knox says, "a revision of the Liturgy being called for, the revisors seized the opportunity contrary to what the public was reckoning upon, to make our formularies not more Puritanic but more Catholic." Dr. Cardwell admits that "there was a distinct and settled desire to exclude the Puritans from the church." Baxter says they "made things far harder and heavier than before." Baxter, part ii. pp. 369, 384, 427. Knox's Remains, vol. i. pp. 59-61.

† Letter from a person of quality. 1675.

exultation cried, "We have carried it for Bel and the Dragon."* One of the alterations caused much profane jesting. The prayer for the High Court of Parliament was now introduced into the Prayer Book, in which prayer the king is styled "our most religious king." This expression gave great offence, and must have astonished the profligate king and his witty friends, who "often asked him what must all his people think when they heard him prayed for as their most religious king."† Besides marks of an angry anti-Puritan spirit, our Prayer Book bears traces of the haste with which it was pushed through Convocation, for, in truth, "the time was too short for the revision."‡

Under such adverse circumstances was the Prayer Book revised for the fourth time; and has never been altered since.

The Convocation having reviewed the Book of Common Prayer, the next step was to authorise and legalise its use. In order to prepare the nation for the severe measure which was about to be introduced into Parliament, sham plots were got up in several counties; reports were spread about that the Presbyterians were conspiring; the king went down to the House and recommended his faithful Commons to watch carefully these wicked people, "who labour day and night to disturb the public peace."‖ Whereupon Sir John Pakington and some other country squires inflame the House with accounts of the dangerous Presbyterian plots down in Worcestershire and elsewhere. The

---

* The Rehearsal Transprosed, p. 500. Clarendon had, when a Reformer, doubted the propriety of reading the apocryphal books. See his letter to Dr. Creighton, in Clarendon State Papers, vol. iii. p. 335.

† He was known to be a libertine, gambler, and infidel. Guizot's Hist. of the Restoration, vol. i. p. 190. Burnet, vol. i. p. 314.

‡ Lathbury's History of Convocation, p. 390.

‖ Rapin, vol. ii. pp. 627, 629. Mrs. Hutchinson's Memoirs, pp. 391, 392.

fiery Cavaliers were ready for any act of vindictiveness and the common talk amongst the leading churchmen was,—"We will have an Act that shall reach every Puritan in the kingdom, and if any of the rogues stretch their consciences and try to remain in the church, we will insert other conditions and subscriptions." It will be understood that the Act of Uniformity passed in Elizabeth's time, was now in force. Sheldon feared that unless this Act were set aside, many of the Puritans would remain in the church, and for this reason the Earl of Northumberland's proposal, that Queen Elizabeth's Act and the old Prayer Book should be adhered to, was under specious pretences rejected.* Sheldon and his party, therefore, introduced into a new Act of Uniformity clauses which they knew would gall the Puritans, and drive most of them from the church.† In the House of Lords the new Act of Uniformity had neither a smooth nor a rapid progress. Its cruel object was apparent, and though it had, says Ralph, the dead weight of the bishops in its favour, several amendments were carried rendering it less severe. The Lords shewed some concern for tender consciences, and inserted a proviso giving to the ministers who were to be cast out of their livings, one-fifth of the income for their support, following the example of Elizabeth when she enforced her Prayer

---

* The Puritans were quite aware of the prelates motives; they said— The prelates feared that the old conformity would not serve turn; they have added such new materials of set purpose, which keep out a thousand at least that would have yielded to the old conformity. Baxter, part ii. p. 294.

† The bishops instead of using any moderate softening measures had got the Act of Uniformity so worded by Keeling the lawyer, that the terms of conformity were made harder than before." Oldmixon, p. 506. Echard says: "No doubt its severity was promoted by some, to keep out certain, who, they thought, did not deserve to enter the church." Again, "The Act was framed with as much skill and exactness as it well could be, for introducing strict conformity, and excluding those mischiefs that had crept in and overturned the church." Echard's History, pp. 799, 802. Life of Philip Henry, p. 195. Baxter, part ii. p. 384. Clarendon's Life, vol. ii. pp. 287, 292. Calamy's Baxter, p. 170.

Book; Cromwell also, had done the same.* But when the Bill went down to the Commons, Clarendon himself tells us that every man, according to his passion, thought of adding somewhat to it, that might make it more grievous to somebody whom he did not love. The mitigations of the Lords were highly displeasing to the Commons; they rejected them all; nothing should interfere with the fulness of their revenge. A conference between the two Houses followed. The Lords appealed to the king's declaration from Breda, in which he had promised a liberty to *tender consciences*, and that no man was to be disquieted on account of his religion. The Commons resorted to contemptible equivocation and falsehood. They said—"tender consciences" did not refer to the ministers, but to the flocks, the former were misleaders, the latter misled. This bold lie was followed by despicable sophistry; they pleaded that the king had limited his promise to opinions which do not disturb the peace of the kingdom, and subject to the "consent of Parliament." The debate was long; at length Clarendon, who says that he "would have been glad that the Act had not been clogged with many of those clauses," came with the whole power of the Court to the aid of the Commons. The Lords gave way, and the Bill finally passed by a small majority.† The Act was to come into operation on St. Bartholomew's Day following (August 24th, 1662). This day was chosen for the malignant purpose of depriving the ministers of the year's income, as the

* Collier, speaking of Cromwell's Act, says, "It must be said, these usurpers did not plunder and persecute without some resemblance of compassion; for, by the Act, a fifth part of the profits of the benefice is allowed to the wives and children of ejected ministers." The fifth, however, was not always paid. See Bishop Hall's Hard Measure. Heber's Life of Jeremy Taylor, p. 20. Collier, vol. viii. p. 375. Baxter, part i. p. 97.

† Ralph's Hist., vol. i. p. 59. Clarendon's Life, vol. ii. pp. 286-296, 302. Burnet, vol. i. p. 317. Oldmixon, p. 506. Lingard's History, vol. xii. pp. 44, 45.

tithes were due at Michaelmas (September 29th).* Thus were the solemn promises of Clarendon and Morley that there should be moderation and charity,—thus were the declarations published by the Royalists, that all animosities should be forgotten, no uncharitableness retained, and no revenge attempted,—thus were the promises of the king to the Presbyterians that he would impose no hard conditions upon their consciences,—thus was the Declaration from Breda, the compact between the king and the Presbyterians, the royal charter, on the faith of which Charles had ascended the throne,—shamefully violated.† Not only was the Act of Uniformity a violation of promises and pledges, an unwise and wicked retaliation most alien to the spirit of Christianity; it was revenge taken upon men, few of whom were responsible for any severities which had been suffered by the Anglican clergy, and certainly had been the chief instruments in placing the king upon the throne. They had kindled the loyalty of the nation, prayed, exhorted, and fought for Charles, when the Cavaliers could not, or would not, raise an arm. Charles, when annoyed with the bishops, did not hesitate to taunt them with their ingratitude to the men to whom they owed their restoration to power.‡

* Although the Commons were such violent haters of the Puritans, they were not favourable to Laud's opinions and practices; for, suspecting, not without reason, that the alterations which the clergy had been making in the Prayer Book were in that direction, a motion was made that they should be debated, and it was only by the narrow majority of six that they were allowed. Journals of the Commons, April 16th, 1662. See also Proctor on the Book of Common Prayer, p. 132, note 3, and page 133, note 2.

† The king was restored "more perhaps upon the confidence of his declarations and promises from Breda, than any other human means." Preface to the first edition of Clarendon's Hist., 1702. That Charles recognised the Declaration from Breda as a compact is proved by his speech, July 8th, 1661, in which he also reminds the Commons of the declaration which many of them had made, to renounce all animosities. Clarendon's Life, vol. ii. p. 261.

‡ Clarendon's Life, vol. ii. p. 475. Baxter, part ii. p. 340. Echard's History, p. 771. Lingard, vol. xii. p. 107.

The famous Andrew Marvell, who was a member of this Parliament, has given us his opinion of the conduct of the leading churchmen at the Restoration. Writing about 1672, he says: "If there had been a little moderation and temper, the Nonconformists could not stick out; but so far from moderation, some contrived that there should be no abatement; on the contrary, several unnecessary additions were made, only because they would be more ungrateful to the Nonconformists. To shew that they were *cunning*, even *revengeful men*, they drilled things on, till they procured a law, wherein, besides the conformity of former times, new conditions were imposed on holders of livings, such as they knew that the Nonconformists would rather forsake their livings than swallow."* The remark of one of the ejected clergy on the Act of Uniformity is worthy of notice. He said, "Before the wars [between the king and Parliament] the Puritans generally made a shift to conform and come into the Church, notwithstanding the hard usage they foresaw they were likely to meet with; but to prevent this afterwards, the new barriers or fortifications were erected by the Act of Uniformity to keep them out." Locke writes to the same effect, and the opinion of this philosopher will be conclusive with all, save the successors of Lauds and Sheldons,— "That Bartholomew-Day was fatal to our church and religion, throwing out a very great number of worthy, learned, pious, and orthodox divines, who could not come up to the things in the Act of Uniformity."† Bishop Warburton condemned the Act of Uniformity as opposed to the spirit of the gospel. He says, "It would be hard to say who are most to blame, those who oppose established authority for things indifferent, or that authority which rigidly insists upon them, and will abate

* The Rehearsal Transprosed, p. 212.
† Letter from a person of quality. 1675.

nothing for the sake of misinformed consciences. I say it would be hard to solve this, had not the apostle done it for us, where he says, 'We that are strong ought to bear the infirmities of the weak, and not to please ourselves.' I myself, says he, do so, and all for the gospel's sake. This is the man who tells us he had fought a good fight, and overcome. And we may believe him, for in this contention he is always the conqueror who submits."* The clauses introduced into the Act of Uniformity to expel the Puritans were these :—

I. All persons having any cure of souls or ecclesiastical dignity, were to be ordained by a bishop. This was a new feature in the church of England, says Clarendon, for there had been many holding benefices, in the most flourishing time of the church, who were ordained in France and Holland. The Puritans, who had entered the ministry during the wars, had been ordained by presbyters, and to re-ordination they strongly objected. When Morley was negociating with the Presbyterians before the Restoration, he had suggested an expedient, to which probably most of the Puritans would have consented; and in the Lords, when this clause was being debated, it was urged in defence that the hypothetical form might be used. But nothing more was heard of these expedients.†

Lord Shaftesbury in 1675, speaking of the Act of Uniformity, said, "We unchurched all the foreign Protestants that have not bishops, though the contrary was both allowed and practiced from the beginning of the Reformation, till this

---

* Marsden's Hist. of the later Puritans, p. 456.
† Bramhall, the Primate of Ireland, was displaying tact and some moderation in dealing with this difficulty, and succeeded in winning many of the Irish Presbyterians.   Biographia Britannica, vol. ii. p. 569, note R. Birch's Life of Tillotson, pp. 171, 176. Six years after the passing of the Act of Uniformity, an expedient was agreed upon with regard to the re-ordination by Bishop Wilkins. Sir Matthew Hale, Tillotson, and Stillingfleet, on the part of the church; and Baxter, Bates, and Manton, on the part of the Puritans.

Act, and several bishops made of such as were never ordained priests by bishops."*

II. All ministers and schoolmasters were required to declare "that it is not lawful, upon any pretence whatsoever, to take arms against the king;" and, further, they were to declare that the "Solemn League and Covenant" was an unlawful oath, binding no one who had taken it. The Puritans thought the first declaration to be destructive of the right of self-defence; to be a sacrificing of all that was dear and valuable, their estates, their liberties, their lives, to the will of the prince. They could not renounce "the Solemn League and Covenant," for although some of them had not taken it, and more of them were all along against the imposing it; yet to determine for all that took it, that they were not bound by it, they thought unwarrantable.† These disgraceful political declarations were inserted by the Commons, after long and passionate debates. Clarendon appears not to have approved of them, and tells us, that they added to the displeasure and jealousy against the bishops, by whom they were thought to be prepared, and commended to their party in the Lower House.‡

III. All ministers were required to declare their "unfeigned assent and consent to all and everything contained and prescribed in and by the Book" of Common Prayer. It made a great noise, says Clarendon, and they all "cried out that it was a snare to catch them, to say that which could not consist with

---

* Letter from a person of quality. 1675. Clarendon's Life, vol. ii. pp. 288-290.

† The Solemn League and Covenant, devised by the Scotch Presbyterians and adopted by the Parliament in 1643, had been the tyrannical instrument by which many of the church clergy had been turned out of their livings; it was now used to ruin the Puritans. Burnet, vol. i. p. 313. Collier, vol. viii. p. 262. D'Oyly's Life of Sancroft, vol. i. p. 28. Calamy's Baxter, p. 541.

‡ Clarendon's Life, pp. 291, 292, 303. Baxter, part i. pp. 64, 65, part ii. p. 387.

their consciences." They were content to read the Prayer Book; but declaring their unfeigned assent and consent to everything contained and prescribed therein, would imply, they said, that they were convinced that it was so perfect that nothing therein could be amended. They could not with a safe conscience make such a declaration concerning any *human* composition; nay, they thought a man could not say so much even of the translation of the Bible, which contained, as all allowed, mistakes and faults.* The majority of the Puritans considered that this declaration pledged him who made it, to an absolute approval of and belief in every line and word in the Prayer Book. John Ray, Fellow of Trinity College, Cambridge, who was well known in his day by his philosophical writings, an intimate friend of Tillotson and Bishop Wilkins, in whose palace at Chester he often stayed, being pressed to take a living, declined, saying: "I use the Prayer Book, and approve of it as a form, but I cannot declare my unfeigned assent and consent to all and everything in it."† The ejected rector of Ubley, in Somersetshire, has left his reasons for refusing to make this declaration. He says, that after having read books, meditated, and conferred with others, he betook himself, on August 21st, to extraordinary supplication to God, to guide and establish him. The issue was, that whatever might be the consequences, he could not take the declaration. He was not against forms of prayer, he could use many things prescribed in the Prayer Book: but to declare his unfeigned assent and consent to all and everything contained in it, was what he could not do. Of the Prayer Book, he says: "I bless God it is so good, but yet it might be better. It is true, that I have read most of the Common Prayer Book, and so might do

---

* Clarendon's Life, vol. ii. p. 290. Calamy's Baxter, p. 504.
† Nonconformists' Memorial, vol. i. p. 214. Nicholls's Literary Anecdotes, vol. i. p. 143.

it again ; but it is one thing to read a considerable part and another to declare an unfeigned assent and consent to everything."* The Latitudinarian or Liberal clergy took the declaration, looking upon it as an innocent promise to conform to the Prayer Book.† Patrick, afterwards Bishop of Ely, says in his Autobiography: At Bartholomew's Day, 1662, all beneficed persons were "to comform to the Book of Common Prayer, which I procured and read, *and expressed my assent and consent to the use of it*, August 17th ; and subscribed before the Bishop on the 18th at Kingston." Bishop Morley, talking one day with an ejected minister, asked him why he could not conform : the minister replied, that it was on account of the assent and consent to everything in the Prayer Book ; the Bishop said: "You must not philosophize upon the words assent and consent.—no more was intended than that the person so declaring, *intended to read the book;* and, therefore, if you would make the declaration in the words prescribed in the Act, and then say, that thereby you mean no more than that you would read the Common Prayer, I would admit you into a living."‡

But not only did the Puritans object to this mischievous declaration in which they were abundantly justified if their interpretation was right, they further complained of the shortness of the time allowed them for deliberation. The new Prayer

* Nonconformists' Memorial, vol. ii. p. 381.

† The meaning of this declaration (which is still required from all clergymen) is doubtful, for the Act explains it as an assent and consent *to the use* of all things in the Prayer Book; whereas the declaration itself seems to imply, as Baxter and his friends considered, an entire approval of all its contents. An attempt was made in the House of Lords, July 25th, 1663, to put upon it this explanation, that it "be understood only as to practice and obedience." Not one bishop objected, but the Duke of York (the head of the Roman Catholic party) and thirteen lords protested. The Commons rejected the clause.—See Speaker Onslow's Notes in Burnet, vol. i. pp. 312, 318. Baxter, part ii. pp. 389, 427.

‡ Autobiography of Symon Patrick. Nonconformists' Memorial, vol. ii. p. 24.

Book contained six hundred alterations,—alterations which are allowed to be anti-Puritan and effected stealthily,—and it was so long being printed, that it was not published until August 6th, on which day it was advertised as "now perfectly and exactly printed, the price of which book is ordered to be but six shillings, ready bound." The consequence of this was, " that of the 7000 ministers who kept their livings, few, except those who were in or near London, could possiby have a sight of the book with its alterations, till after they had declared their assent and consent to it."* This is confirmed by Burnet and Locke ; the former tells us that few of the Prayer Books were ready for sale when Bartholomew's Day arrived; many left their livings, as they could not with a safe conscience subscribe to a book that they had not seen; "some made a journey to London on purpose to see it. With so much precipitation was that matter driven on, that it seemed expected that the clergy should subscribe implicitly to a book they had never seen. This was done by too many, as I was informed by some of the bishops."‡ To the same effect is Locke's testimony ; he says, "so great was the zeal, and so blind the obedience, that if you compute the time in passing this Act, with the time allowed for the clergy to subscribe the Book of Common Prayer, you shall plainly find that it could not be printed and distributed, so as one man in forty could have seen and read the Book they did so perfectly assent and consent to."§ Mr. Steele, vicar of Hanmer, in Flintshire, said in his farewell sermon, he was silenced and turned out for not declaring his unfeigned assent to a book which he never saw nor could see.|| Archdeacon Hare speaks thus of this declaration :

* Baxter Appendix, viii. p. 121. Calamy's Baxter, p. 502.
‡ Burnet, vol. i. p. 318.
§ A letter from a person of quality. 1675.
|| Life of Philip Henry, p. 119.

" This straitwaistcoat for men's consciences could scarcely have been devised, except by persons themselves of seared consciences and hard hearts,—by persons ready to gulp down any oath without scruple about more or less." And Hallam says, this declaration seems to " amount, in common use of language, to a complete approbation of an entire volume, such as a man of sense hardly gives to any book."*

* The objections of the Puritans to this mischievous declaration, are justified by the use which Sprat, Bishop of Rochester, made of it. When he was a member of the Commission of 1689 to revise the Prayer Book, one of his objections to making alterations was, that the clergy had given their assent and consent to all things in the Prayer Book. See Diary of the proceedings of the Commissioners of 1689, published by the order of the House of Lords, 1854, p. 96. Hallam, vol. ii. p. 338.

CHAPTER III.

BLACK BARTHOLOMEW'S DAY.—THE 2000 CONFESSORS, BAXTER, HOWE, PHILIP HENRY, GOUGE, SHELDON, MORLEY, GUNNING.—THE MODERATE CLERGY, SANDERSON, PEARSON, JEREMY TAYLOR.

ST. BARTHOLOMEW'S DAY was already famous in the annals of religious bigotry. The Presbyterians remembered that ninety years before had the Protestants of Paris been massacred, and they "compare the one to the other." They had frequent meetings for consultation; and from many a parsonage there went up earnest, solemn prayers to the Searchers of hearts, that He would guide and support them in this time of great trouble. And God gave them grace to witness to the world, that there were men who did not hold with Sheldon, that religion was a matter of policy, but something to be suffered for, and even died for, if there be need. Some of their prayers and meditations are preserved, shewing them to be God-fearing men, and earnest above all things to have a conscience void of offence toward God and man. "The Lord keep me in this critical time;" "Lord, lead me not into temptation," are the devout ejaculations of the holy Philip Henry.* One good man's mother pressed him to conform to the Act, and remain in his living: "Mother," he said, "if I want bread you can help me; but if I go against my oath, and have a guilty conscience, you cannot." Well-meaning friends pressed them to stretch their consciences and think of their families. An Ormskirk man said to his vicar: "Ah! Mr. Heywood, we would gladly have you preach still

* Life of Philip Henry, p. 116.

in the church!" "Yes," said the vicar, "I would gladly preach, if I could do it with a safe conscience." "Oh, sir," replied the man, "many a one makes a *great gash* in his conscience, cannot you make a *little nick* in yours."* The struggle was doubly keen in the case of those who had families. At Baschurch, near Shrewsbury, the minister was Edward Laurence; he had a wife and ten children, eleven strong arguments, he said, for conforming. Neighbours asked him how he would maintain his family, if he did not conform; he replied, "They must all live on Matthew, the 6th chapter, 25th verse: 'Take no thought for your life, what ye shall eat, or what ye shall drink, nor yet for your body, what ye shall put on.'" John Hicks, brother of the well-known dean, said, when asked the same question, "Should I have as many children as that hen has chickens, (pointing to one that had a good number of them), I should not question but God would provide for them all." One asked his wife her advice, the brave woman replied, "Satisfy God and your own conscience, though you expose me to bread and water." Another said, "God feeds the young ravens, He will feed my children." Amongst the papers of Samuel Birch, vicar of Bampton, Oxfordshire, one is found, called, "Humble Address to my Lord, July 30th, 1662." These are some extracts: "I do not beg for riches, honours, great places, or a pleasant life, for myself or mine. I beg Thy grace in Christ that we may be kept from scandal to religion. . . . . . .As for my provision, my God, I never had any considerable estate, and yet I never wanted. I depend on Thy promise, and have reason to trust Thee. My God, I beg thy direction in this great business, and beseech Thee to shew me what is fully pleasing to Thee, and enable me to do it, for my Lord Jesus's

* Nonconformist's Memorial, vol. ii. pp. 102, 230.

sake, my Saviour and blessed Redeemer. Amen."* The rector of Great Bolas, in Shropshire, has thus recorded the result of his thoughts: "I solemnly profess, in the presence of the great God, before whom I must shortly give an account of my words and actions, that, in my most impartial judgment, after all the light that I can get by reading, praying, thinking, and discoursing with above twenty judicious and solid divines of both persuasions, I look upon it my duty not to conform; and whatever becomes either of myself or family, as I cannot force my judgment, so I will not dare to force my conscience."† There is preserved the written soliloquy of the rector of Carsington, Derbyshire, when debating with himself whether he could conform. Thus does he address his soul: "It is not, O my soul, a light matter that thou art now employed in; it is not the maintenance of family, wife, and children, that are the main things in this inquiry;—it is the glory of God, the credit and advantage of religion, the good of the flock committed to thy keeping, thy ministry, thy conscience, thy salvation, and the salvation of others, that must cast the scale and determine thy resolution. I charge thee, O my soul, to lay aside all prejudices, prepossessions, and respects to, or sinister conceptions of, men of the one or the other party. Let the word of God be umpire. Lead me, O Lord, by Thy counsel: make Thy way plain before me; Lord, shew me Thy way, and, through grace, I will say, It *shall* be my way. And canst thou, O my soul, think of laying down thy ministry upon a light occasion? Take heed, lest, if like Jonah thou overrunnest thy embassy through discontent, thou be fetched back with a storm. If men be Pharaoh's taskmasters, and impose such burdens as thou mayst even groan under; if they be only

---

* Nonconformists' Memorial, vol. ii. pp. 288, 303, 320.
† Calamy's Baxter, p. 351.

burdens and not sins, they must be borne, and not shaken off."* Thus does this good man, on this knees in the presence of his God, reason on this question. These are not the words of factious, peevish humoursome men, who rushed lightly and unadvisedly into damnable schism.

As soon as the fatal Act of Uniformity passed, Baxter withdrew from the ministry, preaching his farewell sermon at Blackfriars, London, May 25th, 1662. He retired to the village of Acton, near London, where he remained some years enjoying the society of his friend, the devout Sir Matthew Hale. It was his custom, he says, to preach, between the public services, in his house, taking the people with him to the church morning and evening; Sir Matthew marking, in an open manner, his approval of this course. There, in the parish church of Acton, were to be seen sitting "next seats together," the greatest lawyer of his time, and the author of the "Saints' Everlasting Rest" and more than a hundred other books,—as well as one of the most powerful preachers of the age,—listening to the curate, a weak, dull young man, that spent most of his time in alehouses.† But some of the other leading Puritan ministers made a last attempt to avert the blow, and obtained an interview with the king. Touched by their moving prayers, he told them "he had great compassion for them, and was heartily sorry that Parliament had been so severe towards them," and promised that he would do all he could to protect them. The Presbyterians departed with their spirits raised, and described in glowing terms the kind expressions of his majesty. The king was at Hampton Court, where the Council were summoned to meet three days before the fatal day, to consider the matter. Sheldon, not yet being a Privy Councillor, had not, it is said,

* Nonconformists' Memorial, vol. i. p. 309.
† Calamy's Baxter, p. 591. Baxter's Letter to Mr. Stephens. Baxter, part ii. p. 440.

a summons; he had, however, heard of what was in contemplation; and at the Council the Presbyterians found their enemy.

"The bishops were very much troubled that these fellows should still presume to give his majesty so much vexation," and declared that they were for executing the Act. Sheldon most copiously and eloquently argued against repealing so sacred a law, passed with so much deliberation, and with so great approbation of good men. Clarendon thought the king had better keep his promise, though he was sorry he had made it. After much debate, Sheldon's arguments prevailed. The king retracted his promise, returned to the bewitching company from which it was hard to tear him: the bishops departed full of satisfaction at the king's resolution, and not a little displeased at their friend, the Lord Chancellor's conduct; the law must take its course, and the sword go through the land.*

The fatal day drew near. On the preceding Sunday, the leading Presbyterian ministers—Manton, Bates, Jacomb, Calamy, Mead, and others—preached their farewell sermons. The churches, and in some cases the churchyards, were full; the people crowding round the doors, and clinging to the windows to hear the farewell words of those who had faithfully and zealously ministered unto them the word of life. "What mean ye, to weep and break my heart?" cried out one of the preachers, as he heard the sobs of his congregation. At last the fatal day arrived,—Black Bartholomew's Day, (Aug. 24, 1662,) a day of lamentation, and mourning, and woe,—when 2000 honest, conscientious men, were cast out of the church.† They

---

* Ralph's Hist. vol. i. p. 76. Baxter, part ii. p. 429. Kennet's Hist. vol. iii. p. 257. Carte's Life of Ormond, vol. ii. p. 260. Burnet, vol. i. pp. 263, 331. Rapin, vol. ii. p. 633. Clarendon's Life, vol. ii. pp. 299-304.

† Rapin, vol. ii. p. 632. Burnet, vol. i. p. 319. Preface to Calamy's Baxter. Preface to Nonconformists' Memorial. Echard, p. 302. Baxter, part ii. p. 385.

F

went out not knowing whither they went; they bid farewell to the comfortable parsonage and the pleasant orchard and the well-stocked garden ; but they found in one of the Psalms for the day words which gave them comfort: "I called upon the Lord in trouble, and the Lord heard me at large. The Lord is on my side, I will not fear what man doeth unto me." "Our sins," said Philip Henry, "have made this one of the saddest to England since the days of Edward the Sixth; but even this is for our good, though we know not how, nor which way."* John Locke says, "Bartholomew's Day was fatal to our church and religion, in throwing out a very great number of worthy, learned, pious, and orthodox divines."†

Thus were the Puritans cast out of the national church, and England is this day suffering the consequences of that cruel, treacherous, vindictive, and schismatical Act.

Some of the ejected ministers were for going to Holland, some to the American Colonies, but most remained at home under promise of being favoured. In the pulpits they were reviled as schismatics; on the stage they were ridiculed as canting hypocrites; in the streets they were insulted by the mob. They betook themselves to various employments; some became lawyers, some practised as apothecaries, some were sheltered by the liberal-minded nobility and gentry, and some had to gain a livelihood by hard labour, of which here is one instance.‡ A Wiltshire gentleman, upon his wife lying danger-

---

* Life of Philip Henry, p. 116.

† Echard admits that "It caused great numbers of good as well as turbulent ministers to quit their preferments, that it bare hard on the good. There were some who would by their piety and learning have been ornaments to the Church." Echard, pp. 799, 803. Collier speaks of the ejected ministers in the following charitable language: "The misfortune of their persuasion cannot be remembered without regret;. those who quit their interest are certainly in earnest, and deserve a charitable construction; mistakes in religion are to be tenderly used, and conscience ought to be pitied when it cannot be relieved."—Collier, vol. viii. p. 436.

‡ Burnet, vol. i. p. 333. Neal, vol. iv. pp. 387, 389.

ously ill, sent for the clergyman. When the messenger reached the vicarage, the parson was just going out with the hounds, and sent word that he would come when the hunt was over. The gentleman was expressing his anger at this message, when the servant said, "Sir, our shepherd, if you will send for him, can pray very well; we have often heard him at prayer in the field." The shepherd was sent for, and asked if he did or could pray, to which he replied, "God forbid, sir, that I should live one day without prayer;" upon which he was desired to pray for the sick lady. The gentleman was so struck with his language, that when they rose from their knees he asked him what he had been; the shepherd confessed that he was one of the ejected ministers, and had been obliged to have recourse to this employment for a living. "Then you shall be *my shepherd*," said the gentleman. A chapel was built on the estate, and there the minister preached. He had been educated at Oxford, and known throughout the University as a good Hebrew scholar.* Some of them underwent great sufferings. The vicar of Walton-on-Thames was one, having a wife and four little children. One morning after he had prayed with his family, his children asked for their breakfast; but the poor man had none for them, nor money to buy food. They all burst into tears. A knock was heard at the door, the wife went to open it; the visitor asked her if she was the mistress, and finding that she was, put a paper into her hand; upon opening it they found it contained forty pieces of gold, and soon after a man came with a horse-load of provisions. They never knew their kind benefactor. A similar circumstance occurred to Henry Erskine; he was the youngest of thirty-three children born to his father. After his ejection from a living in Northumberland, one morning his family were quite

* Nonconformists' Memorial, vol. ii. p. 503.

without food. Whilst the father was endeavouring to comfort them, they heard a man outside calling them to help him off with his load, upon which they went out, took the sack from the horse's back, and found it full of meal and flesh.* Many hundreds of the ministers, Baxter tells us, with their wives and children, had neither house nor bread. A churchman, living at the time, gives us this account: "Though they were as frugal as possible they could hardly live; some lived on little more than brown bread and water; many had but eight or ten pounds a year to maintain a family, so that a piece of flesh has not come to one of their tables in six weeks' time; their allowance could scarce afford them bread and cheese. One went to plough six days, and preached on the Lord's Day. Another was forced to cut tobacco for a livelihood." Brief and vivid is the description which Howe gives of their sufferings: "Many of them live upon charity; some of them with difficulty getting, and others (educated to modesty) *with greater difficulty*, begging their bread."†

Numerous acts of kindness towards the ejected ministers were shown by clergy and laity. It is highly honourable to the nobility, that many of them were averse to the harsh treatment of the Nonconformists. A nobleman, speaking of the declaration of assent and consent required by the Act of Uniformity, said: "I confess I should scarcely do so much for the Bible, as they require for the Common Prayer." Another, after trying in vain to persuade a clergyman to remain in his living, said, with a sigh, "I wish it had been otherwise, but they were resolved either to reproach you or undo you." Several of the ejected ministers found a home in the mansions of the nobility, or were supported by the gifts of their wealthy

---

* Nonconformists' Memorial, vol. ii. pp. 254, 452.
† Life of Howe, p. 160.

friends. Some of the clergy displayed a generous spirit towards the ejected ministers; in several cases the new incumbent being unmarried, allowed his predecessor to remain in the vicarage, and became his lodger. Edward Stillingfleet, then rector of Sutton, in Bedfordshire, sheltered at least one of the ejected ministers in his rectory; for another, he took a large house in his parish, and converted it into a school, where he taught for some years; others he helped in various ways.

Of course, amongst 2000 men there were various opinions. The majority would have been satisfied with a few concessions, which the church could have made without sacrificing her doctrines or discipline; one-half would have remained in the church, as the earlier Puritans had done, if no fresh burdens had been laid upon them; some were violent, whom the church could not gain without giving up her Liturgy and her Episcopal polity. The friends of the Puritans have not failed to censure their faults. Sir Matthew Hale condemned their tendency to attach too much importance to little matters, "They were good men, but they had narrow souls." Tillotson thought they placed "too much religion in little distinctions and singularities;" they were "honest and sincere in the main, and at the bottom, though misled and held under almost invincible prejudices." We may agree with Locke, that they were "worthy, learned, pious, and orthodox divines," but neither the early nor the later Puritans, had shewn themselves to be men of enlarged minds.*

It will help towards forming a right estimate of the exceeding sinfulness of Sheldon's conduct, if something is said of the

* Even Mrs. Hutchinson accuses them of esteeming the cut of the hair, dress, &c., of more importance than due. One of them would not allow her husband to be religious, "because his hair was not in their cut, nor his words in their phrase, and he would continue a gentleman." Memoirs, pp. 99, 143. See the notes to Hudibras, canto i. lines 9, 109. Burnet's Life of Sir Matthew Hale. Birch's Life of Tillotson, p. 399.

leading Puritans, whom he drove out of the church. Their leader was Richard Baxter; yet he was deficient in several qualities needed for such a post. He was too hasty, too fond of nice and subtle distinctions. Patient Dr. Sanderson,—as Isaac Walton calls him,—a man inclined to mild measures, complained of his conduct at the Savoy Conference:* and Clarendon said to him, "If you had been as fat as Dr. Manton, all might have gone on well;" to which Baxter replied, "If your lordship could teach me the art of growing fat, you should find me not unwilling to learn by any good means."† Burnet says, that "he was most unhappily subtle and metaphysical; and Tillotson thought him too much bent on making his own opinions "the rule and standard for all other men's." We can understand from these testimonies, that Baxter had "an unfortunate propensity for multiplying and aggravating the points in dispute." But his failings are as nothing, when compared with his great and noble qualities. As a preacher, Baxter had no equal;—(except that tinker, to hear whom prate, twelve hundred people would gather together early in the dark winter mornings,—John Bunyan); his eloquence was of the most fervid and impassioned kind, which has caused it to be compared to a tempest. He wrote more sermons, engaged in more controversies, and wrote more books, than any Nonconformist of his age. He belonged to no party, sided with no faction, but describes himself as a mere catholic, owning good wherever he found it; he was neither

* Life of Dr. John Owen, p. 107. Life of Sanderson, in Wordsworth's Ecc. Biog. vol. iv. p. 458.

† In 1680, Bishop Lloyd invited Howe to meet him, in order to ascertain what concessions would satisfy the Nonconformists. Howe asked if he should bring Baxter with him? But this the Bishop positively forbade. Howe then proposed Dr. Bates; and was answered, "that no man could be more proper." Life of Howe, p. 271. Baxter, part ii. pp. 364, 365.

a Calvinist nor an Arminian. Churchmen did not like him, because he would not conform to the church ; and Dissenters considered that he was too favourable to the church. He was a man of a most comprehensive spirit ; he thought that the Lord's Prayer, the Creed, and Ten Commandments, contained all that is necessary to salvation.* To shew his Catholic spirit, he said, he would hold communion with all branches of the church, if no sinful act were made a condition; so he would go occasionally to the churches of the Lutherans, Greeks, or Abassines, if he were in those countries.† On the subject of oaths and declarations, his views were enlightened ; he thought them "snares to the conscience ;" it were better for men not to take them, but when taken, men should be careful to keep them.‡ He was honoured by Archbishop Usher ; Sir Matthew Hale and Boyle were his dear friends ; and men of all parties speak of his writings in the highest terms.§ Doddridge says : "Baxter is my particular favourite. It is impossible to tell how much I am charmed with the devotion, good sense, and pathos, which is everywhere to be found in him." Bishop Wilkins says : "Mr. Baxter had cultivated every subject he had handled, and if he had lived in the primitive times, he had been one of the Fathers of the Church." When Boswell asked Dr. Samuel Johnson what works of Baxter he should read, the doctor answered, "Read any of them, they are all good." Isaac Barrow, pronounces

* Baxter says of himself, that he plunged very early into controversies, reading the schoolmen, which were suited to his disposition, Aquinas, Scotus, Durandus, Ockam, and their disciples. Part i. pp. 6, 97 ; part iii. pp. 103, 182. Burnet, vol. i. p. 309. Birch's Life of Tillotson, p. 401. Neal, vol. iv. p. 347.

† Baxter, part i. pp. 64, 65, 130, 133 ; part ii. pp. 198, 437.

‡ "Needless oaths, and covenants, and professions are more useful to Satan as engines to tear, than to the church as means of concord." Baxter, Appendix, p. 132.

§ His works are stated by Calamy as more than 120, besides prefaces to various books. Baxter, part i. p. 114 ; Appendix, p. 123.

this judgment: "His practical writings were never mended, and his controversial ones seldom confuted."*

Although Baxter was the man to whom the Presbyterians paid most deference, he seems not to have been so highly esteemed by churchmen as Manton, or Bates, or Calamy.† Dr. Manton, a round, plump, jolly man, was more popular with the church party than lean Baxter; he was rector of St. Paul's, Covent Garden, London, and, like Dr. Bates, "was high in the esteem of the Earl of Bedford, Earl of Manchester, and other noble persons." Archbishop Usher called him "a voluminous preacher;" his sermons were long and sometimes above the people. On one occasion he had been preaching before the Lord Mayor, and was walking home in the evening, when a poor man followed him, and asked him if he was the gentleman who had preached before the Lord Mayor. He replied, he was. "Sir," said the man, "I came with hopes of getting some good to my soul, but I was greatly disappointed, for I could not understand a great deal of what you said; you were quite above me." The doctor replied with tears, "Friend, if I did not give you a sermon, you have given me one, and by the grace of God, I will never play the fool to preach before my Lord Mayor in such a manner again."‡ He

---

* Grainger's Biog. Hist. and Biog. Brit. Article, Baxter. Judgment of several learned men concerning the Rev. Mr. Baxter.

† Baxter has been disparaged by some churchmen, and despised by dissenters. Echard says: "Baxter was inferior to several of his brethren in temper, judgment, and learning." Echard, p. 787. Kennet says: he was "by education much inferior to many of his other brethren." Kennet, vol. iii. p. 253. Mr. Palmer, the writer of the Nonconformists' Memorial, complains of "those more knowing dissenters, who cannot mention the name of Baxter without a sneer, nor hear him quoted without the suspicion of heresy." vol. ii. p. 542.

‡ Lord Bolingbroke, writing to Swift, says "My next shall be as long as one of Dr. Manton's sermons, who taught my youth to yawn, and prepared me to be a High Churchman, that I might never hear him read, nor read him more." Athenæ Oxon. Grainger's Biog. Hist. Nonconformists' Memorial, vol. i. p. 140.

died in 1677, his funeral being attended, according to one who was present, "with the vastest number of ministers of all persuasions, that ever I saw together in my life, walking in pairs, a Conformist with a Nonconformist."* Dr. Bates was rector of St. Dunstan's-in-the-West, London, and was considered the most polished preacher of his day. He might have had any bishopric in the kingdom, if he would conform. "He had a catholic spirit, and was for an union of all visible Christians, upon moderate principles and practices. As long as there was any hope, he made vigorous efforts for a comprehension." Calamy was more followed than any other London minister. His week-day lecture "was attended by many persons of the greatest quality; there being seldom so few as sixty coaches." He had a chief hand in the restoration of the king, but was flung into Newgate and suffered indignities, like many of his brethren.

Amongst the moderate men who were driven out of the church on St. Bartholomew's Day, there was no one superior to John Howe for intellectual gifts.† He was the minister of Great Torrington, in Devonshire. In his farewell sermon, he told his people, who were all in tears, that "he had consulted his conscience and could not be satisfied with the terms of conformity fixed by law."‡ Whilst chaplain to Cromwell, he had opportunities of serving the persecuted Episcopal clergy; and so unselfish was he, that Cromwell said to him, "You have obtained many favours for others; I wonder when the time is to come that you will solicit anything for yourself or your family." Out of many of his kind acts, one is characteristic of his genial,

---

* Diary of Thoresby, vol. i. p. 7.
† Dr. John Owen was equal to Baxter and Howe in many respects, but the Independents, whose champion he was, did not expect to be comprehended in the Church of England.
‡ Life of Howe, p. 134.

liberal disposition. In 1683, Cromwell appointed a committee to examine all candidates for the ministry. Amongst others who had to come before these Triers, as they were called, was that worthy humourist, Dr. Thos. Fuller. He applied to Howe for advice, saying, " You may observe, sir, that I am a somewhat corpulent man, and I am to go through a very straight passage ; I beg you would be so good as to give me a shove, and help me through." Howe gave him a shove, by telling him what answer to make to one of the subtle questions which the Triers were apt to put, and the worthy Fuller passed satisfactorily.

Howe was remarkable for his " latitude and catholicity ;" his Arminian views caused him to be an object of suspicion to some of the Nonconformists. On one occasion, his friend Bishop Wilkins expressed surprise that he being Latitudinarian did not conform. He replied that it was his *latitude* that made him a Nonconformist.* He was highly regarded by the liberal church divines, Tillotson, Wilkins, Whichcot, Kidder, Fowler, and such men. Like his friends Henry More and Cudworth,—the leaders of the Cambridge or Platonic School,—he was an ardent admirer of Plato, " the great pagan theologue," as he calls him. So much respected was Howe, that when in Ireland, the bishop of the diocese, with the full concurrence of the archbishop, allowed him to preach in any church in the diocese.† It is said of him, " He never made an enemy, and never lost a friend."‡ In all his writings, there is hardly one extravagant or fanatical expression ; his style is bad, but his thoughts are sublime. Never was there a more amiable controversialist than Howe ; Stillingfleet had him once for an opponent, and so charmed was he with his gentleness, that he confessed " he discoursed more like a gentleman than a divine, without any

---

* Howe's Life, p. 106.   † Howe's Life, p. 176.
‡ Even that splenetic party-writer, Wood, has not one ill-word for Howe.   Athenæ Oxon, Howe.

mixture of rancour or sharpness." In 1684, Barlow, Bishop of Lincoln, published a violent address to his clergy, on the necessity of enforcing the laws against the Nonconformists. Howe wrote to him a most beautiful letter, concluding with expressing his belief that he "should meet him [the bishop] one day in that place where Luther and Zuinglius were well agreed."* When he and his brethren were suffering the heaviest persecution, he wrote of his persecutors these words: "I feel within myself an unfeigned love and high estimation of divers of them, accounting them pious, worthy persons, and hoping to meet them in the *all-reconciling* world." How beautiful! The *all-reconciling* world! Such was Howe, the most philosophic, the most majestic of Puritan divines.†

Some writers have considered Philip Henry the most attractive character among the Nonconformists, and admit that his exclusion from the church was one of the evils resulting from the Act of Uniformity.‡ He was the minister of Worthenbury, near Wrexham; a meek, patient, pure-minded man; cheerful under persecutions, forgiving to his enemies; in short, a very faithful follower of his blessed Master. His worst enemies said, his only fault was, that he was a Nonconformist. Before the fatal St. Bartholomew's Day, he spent many days in prayer and fasting; his nonconformity "was no rash act, but deliberate, and well-weighed in the balance of the sanctuary." He read many books, he consulted eminent divines; at Oxford, he counselled with Fell, afterwards Bishop of Oxford; at Chester, he discoursed with the dean and principal clergy, but

---

* It is impossible to describe the gentleness of Howe's letter in reply to Stillingfleet's sermon on "The Mischief of Separation." See Howe's Life, pp. 254 to 266, 311.

† Robert Hall was an enthusiastic admirer of Howe. He said, "I have derived more benefit from the works of Howe, than from those of all other divines put together." Howe's Life, p. 323. Noble's Continuation of Grainger, vol. ii. p. 150. ‡ Carwithen's Hist. Church, vol. ii. p. 327.

found their great argument to be, that if he did not conform he would lose his preferment. This great argument did not satisfy Philip Henry; much less did another. They said, "You are a young man, and are you wiser than the king and bishops?" Wiser than King Charles II., Clarendon, and Sheldon! What presumption! Yet the good man remained unsatisfied, and made this entry in his diary: "God grant, I may never be left to consult with flesh and blood in such matters;" again, "The Lord shew me what he would have me to do, for I am afraid of nothing but sin."* His scruples remaining, he was silenced on St. Bartholomew's Day. "The will of the Lord be done," he writes. His reasons for not conforming were these: He would not submit to be re-ordained;† and he could not declare his assent and consent to everything in the Prayer Book, "for he thought that thereby he should receive the Book itself, and every part thereof, rubrics and all, both as true and good." He thought men ought to enjoy the liberty which Christ has bought, and not to be tied up by "snares and bonds." He would often say, "Oaths are edge-tools, and not to be played with." After his ejection, he attended his parish church and persuaded others to do the same, "for still," saith he, "the Lord loveth the gates of Zion, more than all the dwellings of Jacob, and so do I." For some years he preached only in a private manner, but comforted himself by saying, that he had an opportunity of instructing and exhorting those that were in company with him, when walking to church. As he was regular in his attendance at church, so he was careful to be at "the beginning of the service, which he attended upon with reverence and

* Life of Philip Henry, pp. 109, 117.

† Dr. George Hall, the bishop of his diocese, confirmed him in his objection by his unwarrantable conduct, in requiring the Puritans formally to renounce their Presbyterian orders.—See the debate in the Lords on the clause requiring Episcopal Ordination. Life of Philip Henry, p. 117.

devotion ; *standing all the time, even while the chapters were read.** He diligently wrote the sermons ; always staid if the ordinance of baptism was administered, but not if there was a wedding." If the sermon is a good one, he thanks God for it ; if it is a weak one, he says, " That's a poor sermon indeed out of which no good lesson may be learned." One Sunday afternoon, much was said in the sermon to prove the dissenters schismatics, in a damnable state. When he came immediately after to preach at his own house, before he began his sermon, he said : " Perhaps some of you may expect now that I should say something in answer to what we have heard, by which we have been so severely charged, but truly, I have something else to do ; and so without any further notice taken of it, went on to preach Jesus Christ and Him crucified." When he preached, he usually prayed to God to bless the parish minister, to whom he called himself an assistant in promoting the common salvation of souls. His son, Matthew Henry, tells us that he " was a man of no party ; true catholic Christianity was his very temper and genius."† He used to say, " I am too much a catholic, to be a *Roman* Catholic." The famous saying of Augustine was much admired by him : " Let there be in things necessary, unity ; in things unnecessary, liberty ; in all things, charity ; then, there need not be in every punctilio, uniformity." For twenty-seven years did he pray and labour for conciliatory measures, most earnestly desiring to be restored to the church. At the revolution (1689) he hoped that moderate dissenters would be taken into the church, but when he heard the clergy saying, " As oaths, subscriptions, and ceremonies, were imposed only to keep out such men, they would never consent to their removal to let

---

* Life of Philip Henry, pp. 123, 134.
† Preface to Philip Henry's Life, p. 7.

them in again," he quite despaired, for "he saw himself perfectly driven from them."*

Perhaps a still more remarkable instance of the successful operation of the Act of Uniformity,—["We will have an Act so framed as will reach every Puritan in the kingdom]"—is the case of Thomas Gouge. He had been appointed in Laud's time vicar of St. Sepulchre's, London, where he remained twenty-four years, discharging the duties of that large and populous parish with exemplary zeal and fidelity. It was his practice to catechize in the church, every morning throughout the year, his poorer parishioners, especially the aged, who had most leisure.† He was very diligent and charitable in visiting the sick and destitute, giving away large sums of money. When his parishioners were out of employment, "he set them at work upon his own charge, buying flax and hemp for them to spin, and what they spun he took off their hands, paying them for their work, and then got it wrought into cloth, and sold it as he could, chiefly among his friends, himself bearing the whole loss." Those who were intimate with him say, that they never saw anything in his conversation or conduct, deserving blame. He so much disliked noise, and shew, and stir, in doing good, that if his charities were mentioned, he would rather impute them to any who had the least hand or part in them, than assume anything himself. He was a man of a meek and quiet spirit, always cheerful and always kind, free from all anger and bitterness, ready to embrace and oblige all men ; allowing others to differ from him, even in opinions that were very dear to him. He loved all men who did fear God and work righteousness,

---

* Life of Philip Henry, pp. 193, 195.

† For a full account of this excellent man, see Tillotson's Sermon "at the Funeral of the Rev. Mr. Thos. Gouge." Sermon xxiii. in vol. i. 9th edition, 1728. Baxter, part iii. pp. 148, 190.

however much they might differ from him in things less necessary. When St. Bartholomew's Day came, he could not satisfy himself about the new terms of communion, and retired from his living, saying in his quiet, meek way, "There is no need of me here in London, where there are so many worthy ministers. I may do as much or more good in another way, which can give no offence;" but he continued to attend the church, and employed himself in doing good. "He sustained much loss by the great fire of London, so that he had but £150 per annum left; and even then he constantly disposed of £100 in works of charity." The manner in which he spent a portion of this money, seems rather odd for a schismatic. He, with the aid of some pious friends, causes to be printed, 8000 copies of the Bible and *Prayer Book* in the Welsh language; also the *Church Catechism*, and *The Whole Duty of Man*.* Taking a supply of these books, "he always once, but usually twice, a year, at his own charge, travelled over a great part of Wales, none of the best countries to travel in," to distribute them. Whilst the benevolent old man (past three score years and ten) was giving away Bibles and Prayer Books, Church Catechisms and the Whole Duty of Man, he was excommunicated "for preaching occasionally, though he went constantly to the parish churches and communicated there." What amazing folly! What exceeding wickedness, to drive out of the church these patterns of primitive Christianity!

Turning from these holy men, it will be but just to name the leaders of the two parties in the church, those who promoted and those who opposed the expulsion of the Puritans. The historian of the Puritans, in considering who were the authors and promoters of the fatal Act of Uniformity, gives the first

* Wordsworth's Ecc. Biog. vol. iv. p. 330. The Life of Thomas Firmin, p. 43, Edition 1791.

place to Clarendon, and the second to Sheldon.* Yet it must be remembered that Clarendon did not approve of all the clauses in the Act of Uniformity, was not probably in favour of the alterations made by the bishops in the Prayer Book, and firmly opposed the vindictive efforts of the royalists in other respects. His guilt consists in the deception which he practised on the Presbyterians, in violating the compact made with them in the declaration from Breda, in baffling the Convention-Parliament and procuring the rejection of the Healing declaration, in not restraining the church party, and finally, in giving such men as Sheldon and Morley, their power for mischief. His conduct in civil, was much more respectable than in church matters; for his ecclesiastical measures are a series of political blunders, and evidences of a growing bigotry. His friend, the virtuous Lord Southampton, said of him, "He is a true Protestant, and an honest Englishman, and while he enjoys power, we are secure of our laws, liberties, and religion."†

The Archbishop of Canterbury was Juxon. He was with Charles I. at his death, who called him that good man, and such he seems to have been. The mildness of his temper, the gentleness of his manners, and the integrity of his life, gained him universal esteem; and even the haters of prelacy could not hate Juxon. In the long Parliament, when Bishops were most unpopular, no complaint was made against him; he was never molested, and remained in his palace at Fulham, respected by all. The great and good Lord Falkland was wont

---

* Collier says: "The rhetoric and interest of this great minister [Clarendon] might possibly make an impression on both Houses, and occasion the passing the Act." Collier, vol. viii. p. 434. Neal, vol. iv. p. 379.

† "It is to his memory," says Burnet, "that we owe being a free people, for he with his two great friends, the Duke of Ormond and the Earl of Southampton, checked the forwardness of some who were desirous to load the Crown with prerogative and revenue." State Trials, vol. v. p. 838. Clarendon's Life, vol. 2, pp. 278, 280. Fox's Hist. p. 22.

to say—He never knew any one that a pair of lawne sleeves
had not altered from himself, but only Bishop Juxon; he was
neither ambitious before he became a bishop, nor proud after.*
He was a peaceable man, and told one of the ejected ministers
"he was not for going high against the Presbyterians."†

The man who played the leading part in ecclesiastical affairs
at the Restoration was Sheldon. If at that time Clarendon
carried the crown in his pocket, Sheldon had the keys of the
church.‡ Before the wars he was chaplain to Lord Coventry,
who recommended him to King Charles I. as a man well versed
in politics. His loyalty brought upon him ill-usage from the Long
Parliament; and when at the Restoration, he was placed on the
pinnacle of power, being made Bishop of London, and shortly
after on the death of the aged Juxon, Archbishop of Canterbury, he seemed more intent on revenging his own wrongs,
than healing the church's wounds. It can scarcely be said that
Sheldon betrayed the Presbyterians; yet an honourable man
would have considered himself pledged to fulfil the Royalist
declarations, that there should be no revenge attempted, and all
animosities should be forgotten. And independently of these
promises, we expect to see in clergymen something of the spirit
of Christianity. But Sheldon's conduct at the Savoy Conference,—the Act of Uniformity, the blame of which fell heaviest
on Sheldon,—the unrelenting cruelty with which he hounded
on the clergy by his circular letters, to fresh persecutions of the

---

* Aubrey's Lives, vol. ii. p. 576.
† The character given of him by Sir Philip Warwick, is fully justified
by impartial writers. See Warwick's Memoirs, pp. 100—104. Grainger's
Biog. Hist. Baxter, part i. p. 25; part ii. p. 433.
‡ Isaac Walton, writing about 1678, says that Sheldon was appointed
by the king to recommend clergymen for the vacant bishoprics. Pepys, in
1662, speaks of him as "now one of the most powerful men in England
with the king." Lord Dartmouth says, that he was known to be Clarendon's
creature. Kennet, vol. iii. p. 267. Life of Seth Ward, by Dr. W. Pope.
Burnet, vol. iv. p. 508.

Nonconformists,—are not only shameful violations of the promises made to the Presbyterians, but awful examples of the slight depth to which the spirit of religion had penetrated into his heart. Sheldon had no private vices; he was neither unchaste, intemperate, nor covetous; he was generous, courteous, and affable; his polished manner pleased all who had intercourse with him. Sir Francis Wenman used to say "He was born and bred to be Archbishop of Canterbury."* At the time of the Great Plague (1665) he distinguished himself by his charitable exertions for the poor sufferers. He rivalled in his munificence the great prelates of the middle ages, for his account book, found at his death, shewed that his gifts in seventeen years amounted to the splendid sum of £66,000. As a theologian he takes no position, and in every particular except munificence is inferior to those great divines who make his time the Augustan age of the Anglican church. Though well versed in politics, he was no statesman, being imbued with the passions and prejudices of his day, short-sighted, and narrow-minded. His ruling passion was detestation of the Puritans, whom he considered plagues and pests to the church. His chaplain and panegyrist, Dr. Samuel Parker, tells us that "he freed the Church of England from these plagues for many years," and "guarded every pass and avenue with such diligence" that all the efforts of the schismatics to be received into the church again were baffled.† When the Act of Uniformity was being discussed, the Earl of Manchester said, "I am afraid the terms are so hard that many of the ministers will not comply." Sheldon replied, "I am afraid they will." On another occasion, when

* Clarendon's Life, vol. i. p. 49.

† Burnet says, that the blame of all this fell heaviest on Sheldon. Oldmixon also speaks of Sheldon as the prime mover in the Act of Uniformity. "To him the Protestant religion, and English liberty, are indebted for the Act of Uniformity and other stinging Acts against Dissenters." Oldmixon, p. 515. Burnet, vol. i. p. 319.

Dr. Allen said, "It is pity the door of the church is so strait;" Sheldon answered, "It is no pity at all; if we had thought so many of them would have conformed, we would have made it straiter."* But his schismatical and persecuting policy, sprung more from political motives, and dislike of the manners of the Puritans, than from religious bigotry; for he seemed not, says Burnet, to have a deep sense of religion, if any at all, speaking of it as an engine of government and a matter of policy. He was indifferent to men's theological opinions, saying, the chief point of religion was a good life; if men led upright, sober, chaste lives, then, but not till then, they might look upon themselves as religious; otherwise it would signify nothing what form of religion they followed or to what church they belonged. He did not, says his chaplain, set so much value on prayers as others did; was unwilling to cant much about religion, and liked not people of over strict lives,† whom he had no mind to imitate. Bishop Henchman recommending a clergyman to him for preferment, the archbishop said: "I believe your lordship is mistaken in the man, I doubt he is too puritanical;" whereto the bishop replied: "I assure your grace he is not; for he will drink a glass of wine freely."‡ He was a facetious man, fond of drollery, especially at the expense of the Puritans. When a Mr. Hickeringill was ordained to a cure in Colchester, a place notorious for Puritanism, Sheldon pleasantly told him, that he must break his shins there in breaking the ice, and it was but a just penance for his youthful pranks, in being a soldier

---

* Calamy's Baxter, pp. 170, 181. Neal, vol. iv. p. 379.

† Burnet, speaking of the heavenly-minded Leighton, says: "Sheldon did not much like his great strictness, in which he had no mind to imitate him." Parker's Commentaries. Burnet, vol. i. pp. 235, 303   Biog. Brit. Article, Sheldon.

‡ Nonconformists' Memorial, vol. ii. p. 25.

and seaman, under the two great Hectors of Europe, Cromwell and Charles Gustavus.* During that time of sin and shame, when the court swarmed with women who had no virtue, and men who professed no religion, with Barbara Palmers and Nell Gwynns, Buckhursts and Sedleys, so that a clergyman declared he thought "hell was broke loose," Sheldon was then dispensing splendid hospitality at Lambeth. Every morning the archbishops, chaplains, and gentlemen officers met in a sort of still-house, where a good woman provided them such liquors as they liked best; this room they called their coffee-house. In the common hall of that noble palace, every day a sumptuous dinner was spread; bishops and persons of quality were there, the high tory magnates of the day, secretaries of state, judges, his grace's chaplains and officers. After the good cheer, the archbishop rose, and retired to his withdrawing room; the chaplains and gentlemen officers to their lodgings to drink and smoke.† It was a favourite amusement in those days to mimic the Puritans. Pepys, dining at Lambeth, witnessed a performance of this kind. He says, "A noble house, and well-furnished with good pictures and furniture, and noble attendance and good order, and a great deal of company though an ordinary day; and exceeding great cheer, nowhere better, or so much, that ever I think I saw for an ordinary table. . . . . . Most of the company gone, and I going; I heard by a gentleman of a sermon that was to be there, and so I stayed to hear it, thinking it serious, till by and by the gentlemen told me it was a mockery, by one Cornet Bolton, a very gentleman-like man, that behind a chair did pray and preach like a Presbyter Scot, with all the possible imitation in grimaces and voice, and his text about the

---

* Thoresby's Correspondence, vol. ii. p. 15. Baxter, part iii. p. 141.
† Life of Anthony Wood, Aug. 25th, 1669, Feb. 9th, 1671. Lives of the Norths, vol. i. p. 150, vol. iii. pp. 307, 310.

hanging up their harps upon the willows, and a serious good sermon too, exclaiming against bishops, . . . till it made us all burst; but I did wonder to have the bishop at this time to make himself sport with things of this kind, but I perceive it was shewn him as a rarity, and he took care to have the room-door shut; but there were about twenty gentlemen there."* This is a curious scene for an archbishop's palace; even Pepys, who was by no means puritanically inclined, wondered at it—Cornet Bolton preaching with all possible grimaces on hanging their harps upon the willows, till it made us all burst, our drollery-loving archbishop taking care to have the room-door shut—no more need be said of Sheldon.

Morley was the next most influential man, Clarendon's particular friend, to whose daughter Anne, afterwards first wife of James II., he had acted as confessor from the time she was twelve years old. It was Morley who had been so busy before the Restoration amongst the Presbyterians, talking about moderation and charity, assuring them that all differences would be settled in a National Synod and free Parliament, that the king knew how much they had done for him, and he was "sure they would have no cause to repent of it." Having hugged and caressed the Presbyterians, he, like Clarendon, dropped the mask when it was safe to do so, and went heartily into Sheldon's plans.† He was first made Bishop of Worcester, and in 1662, translated to Winchester, Charles remarking, "he would be none the richer for it." It is pleasant to be able to say, that Morley, as he grew older, professed a desire that the Presbyterians should be restored; and became more moderate, of which several instances are recorded. He could

* Pepys's Diary, vol. ii. p. 342. Baxter, part iii. p. 15. Aubrey's Lives, Article Petty.

† Clarendon Papers, pp. 722, 728, 738. Burnet, vol. i. p. 537.

speak of his old tutor, a noted Puritan minister,* as an "honest man," taking care to add "who is now in heaven;" he would kindly talk to the ejected ministers, and endeavour to win them back to the church. He became averse to persecution, as appears from the following incident:—The zealous mayor of some country town, desiring to distinguish himself during his year of office, consulted the Bishop as to what method he should take, effectually to root out the "fanatics;" the Bishop made no reply, but politely ordered a glass of canary. Our zealous mayor then repeated his question, to which the Bishop gave no particular answer, but ordered another glass of canary. Several times did the mayor put the question, and each time a glass of canary was ordered. At last, when the company who had been present had withdrawn, the venerable Bishop, for he was now grown old, gravely advised the mayor, "To let these people live quietly, in many of whom he was satisfied there was the true fear of God; and who were not likely to be gained by rigour and severity."

Gunning was, after Morley, the most active in the Savoy Conference; he stuck at nothing, says Baxter, spoke the most frequently of all, being a good debater, and a man of extensive reading. His life was strict, and mortified; like Laud he was zealous for the revival of ancient ceremonies, and customs, holy water, lights, &c., saying the church ought to have more ceremonies, not fewer. He was noted as a preacher, being much run after by the ladies, "because," as Charles used to say, "they did not understand him."† Pepys heard him

* Mr. John Dod, author of "Dod's Sayings," who instructed Morley in Hebrew. A sheet of his sayings was often pasted on the walls of cottages in the last century. One of Dod's sayings was, "Sanctified afflictions are spiritual promotions."

† When young North preached before the king at Newmarket, one of the ladies being asked how she liked the sermon said, "He was a handsome man, and had pretty doctrine." Lives of the Norths, vol. iii. p. 312. Burnet, vol. ii. p. 428. Baxter, part ii. pp. 340, 364.

preach on one occasion at St. Paul's, and says, "I did hear him tell a story, which he did persuade us to believe to be true, that St. John and the Virgin Mary did appear to Gregory, a bishop, at his prayers, to be confirmed in the faith, which I did wonder to hear from him."* Gunning was a persecutor to the end of his days; and in his theological zeal, sometimes forgot his dignity. On one occasion he challenged all dissenters to a public controversy, appointing three days for the disputation. On the first day he dealt with the Presbyterians and Independents; on the second, with the Baptists; on the third, with the Quakers, who had collected in such numbers, and railed at him so effectually, that he retreated to his palace, followed by a multitude of people, who plucked his sleeves, crying, "The hireling fleeth! the hireling fleeth!" He would go to the meetings of dissenters to break them up; and once sat on the bench of magistrates at the Quarter Sessions, expecting some dissenters to be fined; but the chairman would inflict no fine, saying to the Bishop, "If we would have good neighbours, we must be such ourselves."

The most devoted followers and supporters of Sheldon and Morley were Henchman, Gunning, Pierce, Barwick, Thorndike, Sparrow, and Peter Heylyn; this last had been Laud's favourite chaplain; his active malice was useful to that prelate in his Star Chamber prosecutions. All of these men had more or less of Laud's vindictive, persecuting spirit.

Of the bishops who took part in the Savoy Conference, Sanderson and Cosins were the most learned. Sanderson, Bishop of Lincoln, had been at the beginning of the wars a church reformer, and was much esteemed by the Long Parliament for his learning and virtue. The lawn sleeves may have lessened, as they commonly do, his reforming tendencies,

* Pepys's Diary, vol. i. p. 126.

yet still he was inclined to moderation.* On the evening after the royal assent was given to the Act of Uniformity, he said to a clergyman who was with him, "that more was imposed on ministers than he wished had been." He sent for a clergyman in his diocese whom he esteemed, and earnestly pressed him to remain in his living; when he found that the clergyman could not satisfy himself on several points, the bishop lamented it, saying, that he was sorry some things were carried so high, "which should not have been, if he could have prevented it."† A short time before his death, "he made it his request that the ejected ministers might be used again; but his request was rejected by them that had outwitted him, as being too late."‡

Cosins, Bishop of Durham, was better acquainted with the Fathers, Councils, and Canons, than most of the church divines engaged in the Savoy Conference; his ecclesiastical views were high, and he said some severe things, but was more familiar and affable than the other bishops, and willing to make some concessions. He was a man of a free, generous disposition, and lived like a prince at Durham, where the cathedral service was maintained in something of its ancient splendour. The richly-embroidered copes and vestments, the tapers and basins upon the high altar, the pictures, troubled exceedingly the Puritanic mind.§ He treated several of the ejected ministers with courtesy and kindness. He expressed

---

* He, with Usher, Hall, Prideaux, Williams, and others, drew up a scheme of church-reform by order of the House of Lords. March 12th, 1641. Collier, vol. viii. p. 198.

† Neal, vol. iv. p. 379.

‡ He died a few months after the Act of Uniformity was passed. Baxter, p. 363.

§ Pepys, writing to a friend in 1682, says, that he had been at Durham, "where the bishop seems to live more like a prince of this, than a preacher the other world." Correspondence of Pepys, vol. ii. p. 62. Thoresby's Diary, vol. i. pp. 46, 61.

to the minister of Bishop's Auckland his willingness to ordain him privately, if he would conform, and in a form to which many Presbyterians had no objection. "When Dr. Cartwright took occasion, in the presence of Bishop Cosins, to reflect upon Mr. Lomax, a Nonconformist minister, which was at that time very customary, the bishop said to him, 'Doctor, hold your tongue; for to my certain knowledge John Lomax is a learned man.'"* In his will these words occur: "I take it to be my duty, and that of all the bishops and ministers of the church, to do our utmost endeavour, that at last an end may be put to the differences of religion, or at least that they may be lessened."†

Dr. John Pearson, afterwards Bishop of Chester, gained the esteem of the Presbyterians, by his conduct at the Savoy Conference. He disputed, says Baxter, accurately, soberly, and calmly, and procured himself a great deal of respect from the ministers; and a persuasion, that had he been independent he would have been for peace; and that if all had been in his power, it would have gone well; he was the strength and honour of the bishops' cause, but the ministers doubted whether he heartily maintained it. An incident occurred during the Conference, which indicates a liberal tendency in this great divine. When Baxter and his party were stating the old Puritan grievance, of being compelled to kneel at the reception of the Lord's Supper, Pearson replied, that the Prayer Book did not exclude those who did not kneel; but Morley would not allow such a

---

* Reynolds, Bishop of Norwich, hearing some young clergymen laughing at one of the ejected ministers, rebuked them, saying, "He has more solid divinity in his little finger, than all of you have in your bodies." Nonconformists' Memorial, vol. i. p. 489; vol. ii. p. 275.

† Cosins was esteemed by the Nonconformists. In the Nonconformists' Memorial, he is called "a prelate of great integrity, how high soever his notions were as to ecclesiastical polity." Baxter, p. 363. Neal, vol. iv. p. 396.

liberal construction, and insisted on the exclusive sense.* Burnet speaks of him in very high terms: "He was in all respects the greatest divine of the age; a man of great learning, strong reason, and a clear judgment." His book on the Apostles' Creed is one of the most finished theological works in our language.†

There were several bishops who disapproved of the Act of Uniformity. Laney, Bishop of Peterborough, visiting his diocese a short time before St. Bartholomew's Day, told some of his clergy that he must enforce the Act, adding, "not I, but the law." He afterwards told a clergyman who had some scruples, that "he could look through his fingers," and he allowed a worthy Nonconformist to continue preaching for some years near his residence. Herbert Crofts, Bishop of Hereford, was a conscientious, charitable, and pious man, "a sincere Protestant, and a true son, if not a father, of the Church of England." He said, "he wished the church doors were wider," and in 1675, wrote a short pamphlet in favour of moderation, which was attacked with fury and bitterness by the High Church zealots.‡

There was at this time no lack of great and good men in the church, whose works are monuments of their piety, their eloquence, their learning. The church had sustained a great loss in the death of Dr. Henry Hammond. Upon the same day on which the Parliament met that restored the king, this devout

* Baxter, pp. 346, 364.

† Pearson edited and wrote a preface to The Golden Remains of the ever-memorable Mr. John Hales, of Eton; in the preface Pearson states that "his high veneration" for Hales prompted him to the work. One of Hales's sayings was: "I would renounce the religion of the Church of England to-morrow, if it obliged me to believe that any other Christians would be damned; and nobody would conclude another man to be damned, who did not wish him so." Athenæ Oxon. Stillingfleet's Irenicum. Rehearsal Transprosed. Clarendon's Life, vol. i. p. 53.

‡ It is called "The Naked Truth." See "Mr. Smirke; or, the Divine in Mode," which is a reply from Andrew Marvell to an attack upon it. Evelyn's Diary, Feb. 20th, 1676; Athenæ Oxon, Baxter, part iii. pp. 109, 175.

Christian and learned divine was taken to his rest. It was intended to make him Bishop of Worcester, and as he was a moderate man, it was thought that he would have been in favour of healing measures; for he said, that twenty years' calamity should have taught men more charity and brought them to repentance and brotherly love.* He held the new high views concerning the divine right of bishops; yet, says Baxter, I took his death for a great loss, for his piety and wisdom would sure have hindered much of the violence that followed.† And it cannot be doubted that such would have been the case, for thus did this holy man pray in his last sickness: "Lord, let no unreasonable stiffness of those that are in the right, no perverse obstinacy of those that are in the wrong, hinder the closing of our wounds. . . . . Mollify all exasperated minds, take off all animosities and prejudices, contempt and heartburnings, and by uniting their hearts prepare for the reconciling their opinions."‡

Of all the clergy, no one had so strong a claim to high preferment as Jeremy Taylor. He had been one of the late king's chaplains, and had suffered much for his loyalty to his church and king, having never bowed the knee to Baal-Cromwell, Baal-Covenant, or Baal-Engagement. In learning, he had only one equal amongst the old clergy, Sanderson; in eloquence, he has never been excelled. Some of his greatest pieces had already appeared, proving him to be the most splendid luminary that had adorned the Anglican church. He was a man of blameless life and ardent piety, and in every way fitted to occupy the highest place in the church; but the writer of the Liberty of

* Burnet, vol. i. p. 304. Fell's Life of Hammond. Baxter, part ii. pp. 210, 338.
† Baxter, part i. p. 97; part ii. pp. 149, 208, 210.
‡ See Hammond's Works for the two excellent prayers composed on his death-bed, given at the end of the first volume, 1684.

Prophesying,—a defence of Religious Liberty, only inferior to the Areopagitica, the most splendid of Milton's prose works,— was banished to an obscure bishopric in Ireland ; whether his liberality or piety were the cause, it is hard to say.*

* Heber suggests that Charles might wish a man of Taylor's piety, at a safe distance ; perhaps Sheldon liked him as little as he did Leighton.

CHAPTER IV.

RISE OF THE LIBERAL OR LATITUDINARIAN PARTY.—SOUTHAMPTON, HALE, WILKINS, BOYLE, TILLOTSON, STILLINGFLEET.—THE CLARENDON CODE.—ATTEMPTS TO RESTORE THE PRESBYTERIANS.—THE LIBERAL CLERGY AND THE HIGH-FLYERS.—DR. SAMUEL PARKER.

THE statesmen and divines who were opposed to the narrow and intolerant policy of Clarendon and Sheldon, were too few to render their opposition effectual, but they were men of great weight, and through their influence, liberal views made steady progress in the Anglican church. The originators and earliest disciples of the liberal or latitudinarian school, from which came forth our Tillotsons, Lockes, and Hoadleys, were,—Selden, whose motto, "Above all things, Liberty," written in the fly-leaf of his books, tells of the unquenchable love of mental freedom, which glowed within him,—Lord Falkland—his friends the immortal Chillingworth and the ever-memorable John Hales,—and Jeremy Taylor, who in his famous work, The Liberty of Prophesying, proves that the fundamental doctrines of Christianity are few, and contained in the Apostles' Creed.*

At the Restoration there was a small band of illustrious men, who had imbibed liberal views,—Sir Matthew Hale, Bishop Wilkins, Cudworth, Henry More, Whitchcot, the Hon. Robert Boyle, Patrick, Tillotson, and Stillingfleet. They were mostly Cambridge men, and generally admirers of Plato.

* Hales's tract on Schism, appeared in 1636; Chillingworth's great work, The Religion of Protestants a Safe Way to Salvation, in 1638; The Liberty of Prophesying, in 1647. Lord Falkland propably derived his liberalism from the continental writers. Aubrey's Lives, Falkland and Hales, Athenæ Oxon and Fasti. Clarendon's Life, vol. i. pp. 53, 92. Hallam's Literature of Europe, vol. viii. pp. 72-80, 105-115, 660. Bayle's Hist. Dict. Daillé. Tillotson's Works, vol. iii. p. 443.

The highest in rank of the more liberal minded men, was the Earl of Southampton. He and Clarendon were the chief ministers of the king, but he is said to have been a lazy man, and let Clarendon have too much his own way. He was a man of high honour, great virtue, and one of the very few Royalists who preserved a just regard for the liberties of the people. He was not believed by the bishops, says Clarendon, to have an affection keen enough for the government of the church; and the disgust which a man of his sentiments must have felt at the proceedings in church and state, is said to have determined him to quit the king's service.* When the king was restored, he wished "the design that had been much talked of during the wars, of moderating matters, both with relation to the government of the church, and the worship and ceremonies;" to be carried out. He was annoyed with Clarendon for giving way to the bishops, and for some time there was a coldness between these two statesmen.†

The most eminent member of the liberal party was Sir Matthew Hale, Lord Chief Justice of England, "allowed on all hands to be the most profound lawyer of his time."‡ He had enjoyed the honour and advantage of being the intimate friend of Selden, from whom he may have derived his aversion to restraints upon religious freedom; oaths and declarations, he thought, entangled the conscience. He was a devout churchman, and for forty years never neglected attending church on Sunday. In his advice to his grandchildren, he says, "At church, let your carriage be decent and reverend; sitting at

* Fox's Hist. of James II. p. 23.
† A pleasing instance of his consistency is to be found in Clarendon's Hist., vol. i. p. 442. Burnet, vol. i. p. 390. Clarendon's Life, vol. iii. p. 788. Fox's Hist. of James II. pp. 22, 23.
‡ These are the words of Roger North, whose Tory principles lead him to depreciate Hale. Lives of the Norths, vol. i. p. 121. Yet see the Examen, p. 530.

sermon with your hat off; kneeling upon your knees at prayers; and standing up at the Creed and Gloria Patri, and at the reading of any part of the canonical Scriptures; this hath been my custom for forty years in all times." On Christmas-day, for which he had much reverence, he regularly received the Lord's Supper, and for many years wrote some verses on the birth of the Saviour to express the great joy which was in his heart. But he was so averse to hypocrisy and cant, that he concealed his private devotions, and would seldom speak about the practical part of religion, which somewhat troubled his friend Baxter, until he discovered the true cause. His most intimate friend was Bishop Wilkins, but he associated with most of the latitudinarian divines; and with Baxter loved to converse on metaphysical subjects. He foresaw the dangers attending the Restoration, and has recorded the evils which would probably follow, in a paper written a few days before the return of the king.* He says, "We are like foolish passengers in a storm, that when the boat reels too much on one side, run all to the other; which doth not cure but increase the danger. At the beginning of the troubles, there was too much splendour and formality, &c.; our ecclesiastical government was too tyrannical and sharp, and our cure was to have none at all." He feared that the Restoration would carry men into insolence and insultation over the oppressed party; that men would become proud, vain, loose and profane, insulting, vindictive, justifying themselves by saying,—"It is but a just retribution,"—and resort to extreme measures. How these fears were fulfilled, we have seen.† Whilst he blamed the Puritans for being too

* See his "Considerations concerning the present and late occurrences, &c., May 13th, 1660." It is given in Williams's Life of Sir Matthew Hale.
† See the two papers Considerations, &c., and Observations, &c., in Williams's Life of Sir Matthew Hale.

eager and warm, breaking the church for little things, he considered that men of tender consciences should not be forced to practice that which they believed to be sinful. He held, as Jeremy Taylor and Baxter, that the fundamental doctrines of Christianity are few and intelligible, and contained in the Apostles' Creed. He censured on the one hand those rash people who unchurch all the reformed churches which have not bishops, revile pious Nonconformists, and cry up ceremonies as if all religion consisted in them; and on the other, those extreme dissenters who cry down the established church as popish or anti-christian, and despise churchmen as formalists, without the power of godliness. The Act of Uniformity grieved him; he thought that many of the Presbyterians had merited highly in the business of the king's restoration, and at least deserved that the terms of conformity should not be made harder than before. It was sad to him, to see so many worthy ministers silenced, the church weakened, Papists strengthened, the cause of piety and love greatly wronged and hindered. He helped the suffering ministers; and abhorred the profane scorn and wit with which the Sheldonian clergy treated them. He was desirous that a new Act of Uniformity should be passed, for, as though he had the gift of prophecy, he said,— "The Act of Uniformity will never heal the English nation."*

Wilkins, Sir Matthew Hale's intimate friend, was the most honest and liberal man, who was raised to the episcopal bench, until the Revolution. He made Wadham College, Oxford, of which he was warden during the Rebellion, famous; and advanced to a high pitch the study of astronomy in the University. At his house met Boyle, Wren, Ward, Wallis, and the other founders of the Royal Society, to make philosophical

* Sir Matthew Hale's "Nature of True Religion." Burnet's Life of Sir Matthew Hale. Baxter, part. iii. pp. 47, 48, 176, 181.

experiments. His works are chiefly on philosophical subjects, one of which on the possibility of a passage to the moon, occasioned the Duchess of Newcastle to say to him, "Doctor, where am I to find a place for baiting at, in the way up to that planet?" Wilkins replied, "Madam, of all other people in the world, I never expected that question from you, who have built so many castles in the air, that you may be every night at one of your own."* At the Restoration he was deprived of the Mastership of Trinity College, Cambridge, to which Richard Cromwell had advanced him. Having married the sister of Oliver Cromwell, and being noted for his liberal principles, Clarendon and Sheldon would bestow upon him no preferment; and thus one of the first philosophers in England was for a time in as low a condition as he could be. But in 1668 the Duke of Buckingham setting up as the patron of Liberty of Conscience, recommended him to the king, who, notwithstanding Sheldon's opposition, made him Bishop of Chester. A person asked Sheldon to recommended him to Wilkins for a place, "No," replied the archbishop, "that I can by no means do; it would be a very unreasonable thing in me to desire a favour from one whose promotion I opposed." I will be no richer, Wilkins was wont to say, and he was as good as his word. The lawn sleeves made no change in him; he remained the same liberal, honest man, opposing persecution, and refusing to join the dead weight as the bishops were called by the anti-court peers. He said to Bishop Cosins, on one occasion, "While you, my lord, are for setting the top on the piqued end downward, you won't be able to keep it up any longer than you continue whipping and scourging; while I am for setting the broad end downward, and so it will stand of itself." He tried to undo the Act of Uniformity, but the bishops were

* Granger's Biog. History.

against him and he gained nothing but their dislike and abuse. Bishop Burnet says, he was a man of as great a mind, as true a judgment, as eminent virtues, and of as good a soul, as any he ever knew. Sir Peter Pett describes him, as an ornament of his University, and the English nation, and one who adorned the gospel itself by his great intellectual and moral endowments. Anthony Wood, with all his Tory prejudices, allows that he was a person endowed with rare gifts, a noted theologist and preacher, a curious critic in several matters, a great promoter of the new philosophy and mathematics, as any of his time; and I cannot say that there was anything deficient in him but a constant mind and settled principles; the great men of the church as Sheldon, Fell, Dolben, &c., did malign him in their discourse, for his wavering and unconstant mind in religion.*

The Hon. Robert Boyle was another eminent member of the Liberal party. He and Bishop Wilkins were the chief founders of the Royal Society; and he devoted his life to the promotion of the new philosophy. He had a profound veneration for the Deity, so that he would never mention His sacred Name without a pause, in which practice he was so exact, that he was not known once to fail in it. His main design in his philosophical researches, was to raise in himself and others high thoughts of the wisdom, greatness, and goodness of the Deity. He thought that Christianity was intended to purify the hearts and govern the lives of men; and therefore loved not those disputes about lesser matters in which Christians were engaged. He spoke with great zeal against persecution on account of religion, and it much grieved him to see the severities practiced towards those who dissented from the church, for though he did agree with the church of England, he

* Athenæ Oxon. Burnet's Life of Hale, Baxter, part iii. p. 22.

was for moderation, and thought that tender consciences ought not to be forced. He had no narrow, illiberal thoughts in religion, and was much troubled at the disputes and divisions among Christians. The liberal design of Boyle and Sir Peter Pett, at the time of the Restoration, deserves to be mentioned. "Mr. Boyle and Sir Peter, discoursing of the severities practiced by the bishops towards the Puritans in the reign of Charles I., and of those which were returned upon the Episcopal divines during the following usurpations; and being apprehensive, that the restored clergy might be tempted by their late sufferings to such a vindictive retaliation as would be contrary to the true measures of Christianity and politics, they came at last to an agreement, that it would tend to the public good, to have something written and published in defence of liberty of conscience." Accordingly, two tracts were written, one by Sir Peter Pett, the other by Dr. Thomas Barlow; the latter was not published, "because as, on the one hand, it would not, how strong soever its reasonings were, be sufficient to restrain the rigorous measures resolved upon against the Nonconformists; so, on the other, it might expose the doctor to the resentment of his brethren."*

Tillotson and Stillingfleet, who at the Restoration were young men, became the chiefs of the latitudinarians as they rose in the church; and were most maligned by the Sheldon party and the Roman Catholics.† In the same year in which the fatal Act of Uniformity passed, re-appeared Stillingfleet's first work, the "Irenicum; or, a Weapon-Salve for the Church's Wounds." The learning, the moderation, the reasoning of this remarkable treatise, make it a masterpiece. In

---

* Birch's Life of Boyle. Athenæ Oxon, Pett; and Fasti, Boyle.

† Stillingfleet was the object of Dryden's sarcasm in the Hind and Panther.

the preface he speaks of the mischief of forcing men to observe rites and ceremonies at which they scruple. "Christ's design was to ease men of their former burdens, and not to lay on more. He that came to take away the insurmountable yoke of Jewish ceremonies, certainly did never intend to gall the necks of the disciples with another instead of it. . . . Would there ever be the less peace and unity in a church, if a diversity were allowed as to practices supposed indifferent? The unity of the church is an unity of love and affection, and not a bare uniformity of practice or opinion. The latter is extremely desirable in a church; but as long as there are several ranks and sizes of men in it, very hardly attainable, because of the different persuasions of men's minds as to the lawfulness of the things required." It was a bold act for a young man, to publish such liberal sentiments as these, when "the road to preferment lay another way;" his merits however were noticed by the moderate church party, for he was appointed by Sir Harbottle Grimstone, preacher at the Rolls Chapel; and Lord Southampton presented him to the rectory of St. Andrew's, Holborn; his next preferment was procured for him by Lord Shaftesbury;* at the Revolution he and other liberal divines were raised to the Episcopal bench.

The Act of Uniformity was to the Nonconformists the beginning of sorrows; in 1664 the Conventicle Act passed, suppressing seditious conventicles, as private religious meetings were insultingly called;† and this was followed by the Five-Mile Act, by which the Nonconformist ministers were obliged to take an oath, "I do swear that it is not lawful, upon any pretence whatsoever, to take arms against the king, &c., and I will not at any time endeavour any alteration of government

---

* See the Bishop of Lincoln's Letter to Lord Shaftesbury, in Lord King's Life of Locke, p. 194.

† Clarendon's Life, vol. ii. p. 421. Hallam, vol. ii. p. 349.

either in church or state." Those who refused to take this infamous oath, and write themselves slaves, were not to come within five miles of any city, corporation, or place where they had preached.* This ingeniously cruel statute, promoted by "our great bishop," as Locke calls Sheldon, was warmly opposed by the Earl of Southampton. He said that no honest man could take the oath required from Nonconformist ministers, for though he had always been firm to the church, yet, as things were managed, he did not know but he himself might see cause to endeavour an alteration. "I will not be sworn," exclaimed our free-spirited English Earl, "not to take away Episcopacy."† Dr. Earl, Bishop of Salisbury, also opposed it; and dying a short time after the passing of the Act, some bigots reckoned his death just for opposing it.‡

The Five-Mile Act is the last of Clarendon's code. He was hated by the Court for his virtues; and his haughty dictatorial conduct had made him a host of enemies. It is remarkable that when this great patron of persecution was disgraced, the Nonconformists whom he had so grievously wronged were not eager for his fall, and some were his friends.§

After Clarendon's banishment,‖ the king, professing a desire

---

* Baxter, part iii. pp. 3-5.

† Burnet, vol. i. p. 390. Baxter, part iii. p. 3. Letter from a person of quality, 1675.

‡ He had been sub-tutor to Charles II., who esteemed him more than any of the other clergy, as he never could hear of or see anything amiss in him; he was a charitable, sweet-tempered, forgiving man. See the character given by Isaac Walton, in his Life of Hooker, of this amiable bishop. Burnet, vol. i. p. 390. Calamy's Baxter, p. 584. Neal, vol. iv. p. 417.

§ Baxter, part iii. p. 20.

‖ Sheldon and those of the bishops who were attached to Clarendon were in disgrace. The following extracts from the diary of Pepys will explain the state of affairs at this time:

Nov. 21st, 1667.—Only three bishops for Clarendon's commitment, Reynolds, Cosins, and another.

Dec. 21st, 1667.—The archbishop (Sheldon) no more at the cabal.

Dec. 23rd, 1667.—Bishops of Winchester, Rochester, and some other to bring back the Nonconformists to the church, Lord-Keeper Bridgman, Bishop Wilkins, Tillotson, Stillingfleet, and Burton on the part of the church; Baxter, Bates, and Manton, on the part of the Presbyterians, had several meetings, and at last agreed upon a scheme, (1668). The particulars were laid before Sir Matthew Hale, who drew up a bill to be presented to the ensuing Parliament, which Lord-Keeper Bridgman promised to support with all his power. But no sooner was it known that such a bill was to be laid before Parliament, than a great outcry was raised by Clarendon's friends that the church was in danger, and about to be undermined and ruined. It was said, that it was below the dignity of the church to offer concessions,—that it was better to have the Puritans out of the church as a schism, than in it as a faction, disturbing it and dividing it,—that no one could tell where concessions would end if once the church began making them. It soon became plain, from this clamour, that the bill would be lost. The Commons met, and after "mightily and generally inveighing" against the project, passed a resolution that no bill for the comprehension of dissenters should be received.* Had this bill been carried, about 1400 of the Puritan ministers would have returned to the church.

great prelates are suspended,—a cloud upon the archbishop,—heavy blow to the clergy.

Dec. 27th, 1667.—(Sir W. Coventry) tells me that my Lord of Canterbury is a mighty stout man, and a man of a brave, high spirit, and cares not for this disfavour that he is under at Court, knowing that the king cannot take away his profits during his life, and therefore do not value it.

Jan. 1st, 1667-8.—They did talk much of the disgrace the archbishop is fallen under with the king, and the rest of the bishops also.

* Collier says: "When the House sat, the Episcopal party crushed the design, and carried a vote against bringing in a bill of this nature." Collier, vol. viii. p. 452. Pepys has this entry, Mar. 10th, 1667-8. "He tells me, he believes the Parliament will not be brought to do anything in matters of religion, but will adhere to the bishops." Parl. Hist. Baxter, part iii. pp. 23-36. Burnet, vol. i. pp. 449, 450, 451. Life of Sir M. Hale, pp. 539, 540. Rapin, vol. ii. p. 653.

In 1670, Morley and some of the other bishops talked about restoring the Presbyterians, but nothing was done. The zeal of the Commons was not yet grown cool; they renewed the Conventicle Act, and made it more severe.* In the Lords, Bishop Wilkins opposed it; the king had asked him to be quiet, but he replied that as an Englishman and bishop, he had a right to speak and vote, and should not conceal his opinion. Sheldon zealously promoted these measures; and on no single occasion do we find him restraining the cold-blooded persecution which was now carried on, a persecution which Hallam thinks may have been more extensively felt than that in the time of Charles I.† But a few years later, the Commons seem to have become aware of their folly, for in 1673, they resolved, without one dissentient voice, that a bill should be brought in for the ease of dissenters; it passed the Lower House, notwithstanding some mournful predictions that the kingdom might be endangered and put in an uproar, that the 2000 preachers and 10,000 more might come with arms in their hands.‡ But it was either defeated in the Lords by Sheldon and his followers, or lost through the prorogation which soon followed. The bishops, according to Locke, were frightened at the progress of Popery, but when their fright passed away, they instructed their party to revive the old persecutions of the Protestant dissenters.||

This was followed by another attempt to restore the Presbyterians (1673). Lord Orrery asked Baxter to draw up some

---

* Baxter, part iii. pp. 83, 84.
† Hallam, vol. ii. pp. 350, 353. Neal, vol. iv. p. 444. Baxter, part iii. p. 74.
‡ See the Speeches of Sir John Duncombe, and Sir John Birkenhead. The former gentleman appealed to know "if there were anything in England of persecution to dissenters." Parl. Hist.
|| Parl. Hist. Collier, vol. viii. p. 457. Neal, vol. iv. p. 536. Baxter, part iii. p. 103. Hallam, vol. ii. p. 394. Letter from a person of quality. 1675.

proposals, which being shewn to Morley, who had again intimated his wish that something should be done to heal the breach, were not approved, and the matter came to an end. A short time after, a bill was drawn up by some leading men in the House of Commons; but when it was shewn to Morley, he urged them to withdraw it.* To prove, however, that he was willing to make some concession, he introduced into the House of Lords a bill to take away the declaration of "assent and consent;" but the other bishops opposed it, and it was lost.† As the danger of Popery increased, Morley and some other bishops professed to be anxious to take in the Nonconformists.‡ Tillotson and Stillingfleet again met Baxter, with Bates, Manton, and Matthew Pool (1675); a scheme was agreed upon which Baxter requested should not be shewn to Morley, "as likest to frustrate it," but to Bishop Pearson, a sober, learned man, and Bishop Ward. But all their labours were in vain, for Tillotson wrote to Baxter saying,—He had spoken to Seth Ward, but found that several things could not be obtained; he was unwilling that his name should be used, for although he most heartily desired an Accommodation, and would always endeavour it, yet it would be a prejudice to himself and do no good; there was no chance of the scheme passing without the concurrence of the king and a considerable part of the bishops, which for the present he saw little reason to expect.§

* This bill, like the preceding one, was to abolish all oaths, declarations, and subscriptions required from the clergy, except the oaths of supremacy and allegiance, and subscription to the thirty-nine articles, according to the 13th of Elizabeth.
† Baxter, part iii. p. 140.
‡ Baxter considered that these professions on the part of Morley were a trick; partly to divert from himself and the bishops the odium which their persecuting proceedings were drawing upon them, and partly to enable him by having a hand in the negociations, to be better able to frustrate them. Baxter, part iii. p. 157.
§ Birch's Life of Tillotson, pp. 43, 44. Memoir of Tillotson, in Wordsworth's Ecc. Biog. Baxter, part iii. p. 157.

In 1680, Stillingfleet invited Howe and Bates, to meet Tillotson and Bishop Lloyd, at his house; the bishop, who had declined meeting Baxter, was unable to attend, and the matter fell to the ground.* The nation at this time was in a highly excited state on the subject of Popery; now came into use the terms Whigs and Tories; the people forbidden to *burn* the Pope, gratified their Protestant zeal by *drowning* him. The clergy thought the knife of the Papists at their throats; and the Commons seemed anxious to make friends with the Nonconformists. They appointed a committee, who agreed to a bill for "uniting His Majesty's Protestant subjects." It was read for the first time Dec. 21st, 1680; but meeting with opposition, another was substituted for it, exempting dissenters from certain penalties, which passed both Houses, and afterwards disappeared in a mysterious manner, the king disliking it.† The objections which were brought against this attempt to draw in dissenters were the same as before; and the foolish old cries were raised.‡ The church was in danger,—it would be pulled down,—concessions would increase the boldness of dissenters, a sort of people not to be ruled or advised by the king or fathers of the church,—once begin to yield, and an utter subversion would follow,—dissenters should be forced to yield to the church, not the church to dissenters. This bill of union was not heartily supported by the Nonconformists, because, says Baxter, they found the bill would not go, or if it passed

---

* Life of Howe, p. 271.

† It was said that one of the king's natural sons was standing by the table playing with it, and that he was told to take it away. Kennet says, "The majority of the House fell in heartily with this bill of comprehension." But Ralph seems to think, from its being introduced so near to the close of the session that "it was one of those parliamentary fire-works that are occasionally let off, only to make a noise and expire." Kennet, vol. iii. p. 382. Rapin, vol. ii. p. 719. Echard, p. 999. Anthony à Wood's Life, p. xcvi.

‡ Parl. Hist., Dec. 21st, 1680.

the Commons, it would have been thrown out by the bishops.*
This was the last attempt in Charles II.'s reign to restore the
Presbyterians. Twenty years had now passed, since the ejection
of the Puritans; and men began to despair: "I have no good
hopes of this matter," Tillotson writes to Robert Nelson, "till
minds of men become more calm."

These schemes of comprehension only aimed at restoring
those of the ejected ministers who were Presbyterian, as the
Episcopal Nonconformists were commonly called. The few
of the 2000 who were Independents regarded with no favour
the efforts of Baxter, Bates, and Manton, whom they knew
were dissenters only in name. They called the Presbyterians
lukewarm temporizers,—men of too large principles,—men who
supt the anti-Christian pottage, though they would not eat the
flesh. The Independents were more rigid Calvinists, more
exclusive in their terms of church communion than the Presbyterians, averse to an established church, but in favour of
Toleration. The Presbyterians, on the contrary, were in
favour of union with the National church, but averse to
Toleration, and probably brought upon themselves additional
suffering by refusing to concur in a toleration of the Roman
Catholics. If we, says Baxter, would have but opened the
door to let the Papists in, we might in all likelihood have had
our part.† The sharp persecutions, however, which the Presbyterians suffered in common with other Nonconformists, from
the Restoration to the Revolution, unscaled their eyes, and
purged out of them the old leaven of intolerance.

The excellent men who promoted the attempts to enlarge

---

* Tillotson, writing to his friend Robert Nelson, says, the Bill of Union pleased neither the bishops nor dissenters. Burnet says: "To the amazement of all people, the Nonconformists neglected the bill." Burnet, vol. ii. p. 267.   Birch's Life of Tollotson, pp. 81, 82.   Neal, vol. iv. p. 561.

† Baxter, part iii. pp. 23, 36, 43, 84.

the church were assailed in bitter terms by their brethren. But the liberal churchmen, though the minority, were in learning and in virtue decidedly superior to their assailants. Their attachment to the church was sincere and strong; their lives were irreproachable, their sermons and writings did honour to the church, and upheld its character in the worst of times. Happily, says Baxter, the parish churches of London had the best and ablest of the clergy in them, especially Stillingfleet, Tillotson, White, Outram, Patrick, Whitchcot, &c. The Nonconformists confessed that the Whig churchmen did the church most service, and the Nonconformists most hurt. A leading Nonconformist, writing in 1680, says: Several bishops and doctors of the church of England, as Dr. Lloyd, Dr. Tillotson, Dr. Stillingfleet, Dr. Patrick, are acknowledged to be persons of great learning, worth, and piety, and uphold the hierarchy and the church. Neal allows that "the Tillotsons, Stillingfleets, Whitchcots, Wilkins, Cudworths, &c., were men of the first rank for learning, sobriety, and virtue . . . . . . but their numbers were few, because the road to preferment lay another way."* They were sneered at as latitudinarians, because they were in favour of allowing liberty or latitude to men in things indifferent. They saw with regret the bitterness with which churchmen and dissenters contended about a rite, a vestment, a gesture; and though they themselves had no prejudices against the decent rites and ceremonies of the church, they would not for the sake of uniformity sacrifice unity. In truth, they had "a lofty disdain of those trifling subjects" which were dividing men agreed in the essentials of religion, and their generous minds longed to see such men as Baxter, Howe, Philip Henry, and Manton, ministering at the altars of the national church.

* Kennet, vol. iii. p. 370, note a. Neal, vol. iv. p. 397.

This was their crime, and for this they were reviled as trimmers,—Grindalizers,—no lovers of the church,*—wolves in sheep's clothing,—designing hypocrites,—betrayers and underminers of the church,—men who smile in your face, when about to cut your throat,—men who handled the church with the hands of Esau, but now speak with the voice of Jacob,—men who trim and trick, play fast and loose,—who under their beloved moderation, in a creeping, whining, sanctified dialect, aim at encouraging and supporting dissenters, and on behalf of their old Puritan friends pimp for bills of union, comprehension or toleration; good had it been for the church of England, and perhaps for themselves too, that they had never been born. The churches of moderate clergymen were conventicles. Moderation was declaimed against with so much zeal and fierceness, that it seemed to be considered the sum of all vices; it was denounced as vile cant,—venomous gibberish,—a word to gull and manage the rabble,—the prescription of spiritual quacks and mountebanks for skinning over the church's wounds,—a harmless gilded word, covering the worst of designs against the best of churches. In such terms were the moderate and liberal-minded members of the church, and their struggles against the intolerant policy of the times, reviled.†

The immediate effects of Sheldon's policy are to be seen in the opinions and practices which prevailed in the church from Black Bartholomew's Day to the Revolution. An inferior body of men rushed into the places of the ejected ministers. The

---

* Wood, speaking of Hales's Tract on Schism, says: "It hath given great advantage and use to some that have not loved, nor are lovers of the Church of England, as E. S. (Edward Stillingfleet) in his Irenicum." Athenæ Oxon, vol. iii. p. 414. Birch's Life of Tillotson, p. 391.

† See South's Sermons, particularly those on "The fatal influence of words and names falsely applied," part i.; and "False methods of church government exploded," in which is the description of a conforming Puritan. Kennet, vol. iii. p. 410, notes *a* and *b*.

liberal clergy were depressed, and benefices heaped by the bushel on the favoured ones. The aspirants for preferment found that the quickest way to rise was to cringe to the bishops and great men, revile dissenters, rail at their liberal brethren, denounce the whigs, and cry up the king. The higher clergy set an ill example, idling in London, dancing attendance at some great man's levee, snatching at every piece of preferment that fell vacant, to add to those they already possessed, leaving their spiritual duties to be performed by half-starved curates.* Bribes for preferment, it is said, were not uncommon.† "All promotions," writes Andrew Marvell, "spiritual and temporal, pass under the cognizance of the Duchess of Cleveland." The bishops offended men by their covetousness; great wealth flowed into their coffers, yet they often held with their bishoprics, a deanery, a comfortable prebendary, together with a good fat parsonage, and perhaps half a dozen sinecures; the drudgery of praying and preaching was left to curates hired at the smallest wages.‡ Charles himself complained of the clergy. He said, there would be no dissenters if the clergy lived well, and went about their parishes, but they were ambitious, scandalous, and covetous; they thought of nothing but to get good benefices, and to keep a good table.§ Learning was neglected. At Hereford and Worcester cathedrals lay valuable manuscripts, untouched and useless; the clergy cared not for

* Lives of the Norths, vol. ii. p. 246. Baxter, part iii. p. 147. Whiston's Memoirs of Dr. Clarke.

† An instance is given in Nelson's Life of Bull. Marvell says, too many of the clergy are reported to do this. See the account of Bishop Wood in Athenæ Oxon, and D'Oyly's Life of Sancroft.

‡ Sir Thos. Brown's works, vol. i. p. 203. Marvell's Letters to his Constituents. Basire's Correspondence, pp. 230, 231. Baxter, part iii. p. 141.

§ Baxter's letter to Mr. Stephens. Ellis's Original Letters, 2nd series, vol. iv. p. 26. Burnet, vol. i. p. 448. Pepys's Diary, Feb. 16th, 1668. Locke's Journal, Aug. 2nd, 1680.

such things.* The scholars at Oxford spent their time in ale-houses, taverns, and coffee-houses; learning declined in the University, but drinking and Toryism flourished. One of the colleges was inhabited only by a few families, to keep it from ruin. The Whigs regarded Oxford as a dangerous place, and feared to send their sons, lest they should become Papists and Tories. A Mr. Parkinson was expelled for Whiggism; Locke was basely deprived of his studentship; and the Whigs run down. Drunken riots were too frequent.† White Kennet, then a noted Tory, found one evening some scholars engaged in a drinking bout, whom he reprimanded for keeping such late hours; one of them said suddenly, "You will excuse us; we were now met to drink prosperity to the church; to which *you* can have no objection." He answered with a solemn air, "We are to pray for the church, and to fight for the church, but not to drink for the church."‡ The most servile doctrines were preached; the king was above the law; the people were his property whom he might rob, wrong, and slay, as he pleased. To say that "the anointed of the Lord, the breath of our nostrils," who is "not only the ordinance, but the gift of God," might be resisted on any pretence whatever, was impious, infamous, seditious, heretical, damnable, blasphemous.§ Sprat, the pliant Bishop of Rochester, called Charles II., a god-like man. The most enlightened clergy, as Tillotson and Burnet, thought it not lawful, on any occasion, to take up arms against

* Aubrey's Lives, vol. ii. pp. 556, 557. Hearne's Account of Anthony à Wood.
† Anthony à Wood's Life, pp. 73, 76, 79, 80, 87, 88, 89, 91, 94, 97, 98, 99, 105. Athenæ Oxon, Parkinson.
‡ Nicholls's Literary Anecdotes, vol. i. p. 393.
§ See "The judgment and decree of the University of Oxford," July 21, 1683. Address of the University of Cambridge, Sept. 18th, 1680. Form of Prayer for Sept. 9th, 1683. Kennet, vol. iii. p. 410. South's Sermon "on the Martyrdom of Charles I., preached shortly after the Restoration." Baxter, part ii. p. 367.

the king, and in vain tried to bring the partriotic Lord William Russell to their mind.* The Prayer Book was made an idol, as though "it had dropped down from heaven, and had been framed by a synod of archangels." One divine declared "that there was not one tittle of it, but it was dictated by the Holy Ghost," proving his assertion from the first prayer in the Marriage Service.† To inflame men's minds against Whigs, moderate churchmen, and dissenters, was to act "as true sons of Holy Mother Church." The Tory clergy abhorred, as they did the devil and his angels, those troublesome folks, the Whigs, who cantingly professed to love the king, but would not give him money.‡ The Puritans were an inexhaustible subject of merriment, not in conversation only, but even in the pulpit. Their demure looks, their up-turned eyes, their squinting, their hands crossed upon the breast, their wry mouths, their affected gesticulation, their nasal twang, their groanings, their canting phrases, their hypocrisy, were topics on which the high-flying royalists were never weary of dilating. The sermons were full of girds against the snivelling saints,—the precise fellows, who like pharisees, made long prayers, and felt the pulse of a holy sister.§ These schismatics, fanatics, rebels, must be dealt with

* Lord John Russell's Life of Lord William Russell. Granger's Biog. Hist., Sprat.

† A certain good archdeacon went about town and country preaching from the text, "The cloke that I left at Troas. . . . , and the books, but especially the parchments;" in which he found the whole Liturgy, the Canonical habits, and all the equipage of a Conformist. The Rehearsal Transprosed, p. 166.

‡ Life of Dr. John North, vol. iii. p. 358. Sir M. Hale's Nature of True Religion.

§ The sermons of the witty but profane South, abound in sarcasms against Puritans and moderate churchmen. See those "On confidence in Prayer," "Good intentions no excuse for bad actions," and "The duties of the Episcopal function." See also the letter from Dr. Wallis to Boyle, giving an account of the proceedings at Oxford at the opening of the Sheldonian Theatre. Evelyn's Diary, July 9th and 10th, 1669. Thoresby's Diary, vol. i. p. 53. Fasti Oxon.

rigorously, chastised and scourged, fined, imprisoned, ruined, banished; to introduce them into the church, would be to bring back a plague into her bowels, to tolerate them was to permit a plague to rage around her. They were seditious,— the devils proxies,—a generation of vipers who may rend again the bowels of Church and State,—notorious seducers fit to be transported.* "Cure them," said a preacher before the House of Commons, "by vengeance, teach them by scourges or scorpions, and open their eyes with gall."† But the magistrates after a time grew weary of persecuting the dissenters. Twelve or thirteen of the bishops dining with the Sheriff of London, the conversation was about the dissenters, and the necessity of rigorously executing the laws against them, upon which the Sheriff said: "We cannot trade with our neighbours one day, and send them to gaol the next."‡ The Vicar of Newcastle, writing to a friend says: "I verily beleeve that my endeavour to suppresse conventicles both by preaching and complaining, and writing, is the originall of that disgust which I dayly heare the magistrates have conceived against mee."||

A leading man among these fiery divines, a man in whom Sheldon delighted, was Dr. Samuel Parker. He had been bred among the Puritans. At Oxford, he was "one of the straitest of the sect;" at Bess Hampton's prayer meetings and

---

* Thoresby's Diary, vol. i. pp. 29, 34, 62, 73, 109, 143; vol. ii. p. 419. Basire's Correspondence, p. 232, 233, 271-273, 277, 279.

† The Bible was thought to justify such violence. The Vice-Chancellor of Oxford (about 1670) came to a fanatic's house, and found people praying: he bade them attend St. Mary's Church in the king's name, (the beadle said he would drive them in the devil's name) saying, he had thus converted hundreds into churchmen at Reading. The people reason with him, upon which the Vice-Chancellor justified himself by these words: (Luke xiv. 23) "*Compel* them to come in, that my house may be filled." See Milton's Civil Power in Ecc. Causes. About 1672 the Recorder of London openly said, that it would never be well in England until the Spanish Inquisition was set up. Baxter, part iii. pp. 141, 142, 177, 187.

‡ Calamy's Baxter, p. 607.

|| Basire's Correspondence, pp. 279, 280.

sermons, no one was more constant. He was a rigid faster, and belonged to the *grewellers*,* and was esteemed one of the preciousest young men in the University. Coming to London about the time of the Restoration, he found Puritanism going out of fashion; in a short time his eyes were opened, and as he pretended, he was delivered from the unhappy prejudices under which he had been labouring, for which he gave God thanks. This ecclesiastical weathercock now veered completely round, and henceforward became a great *droller* upon the Puritans. His first production appeared in 1665, which he dedicated to Sheldon, and was rewarded by being appointed one of his chaplains; he was thus placed on the high road to preferment. In 1669, our chaplain wrote a virulent book against the Dissenters, which was followed by his advance to the Archdeaconry of Canterbury. In 1671, he published his defence of this last work, and was rewarded with another piece of preferment, being made Prebendary of Canterbury. In 1672, a still more scurrilous attack on Nonconformists appeared,†—the substance, it is said, of sermons preached at Lambeth, and in the same year he was rewarded by the Archbishop with the rectories of Ickham and Chartham, Kent. Prosperity made the man insolent; "if he chance but to sneeze, he prays that the foundations of the earth be not

---

* Bess Hampton was an old lady, at whose house in Oxford many rigid young Puritans were in the habit of meeting. They were called "grewellers," because of their "feeding on thin broth, made of oatmeal and water only." Athenæ Oxon. Parker.

† He now met with a man more than his match in wit, the famous Andrew Marvell, who, disgusted with his insolence, "took him to task, to clip his wings." Marvell handled him so successfully, that from the king down to the tradesmen, all were laughing at Parker. Mortified at his defeat, he withdrew from town, and wrote nothing more until Marvell was dead. Mr. Carwithen says: "It is the opinion of Whigs only, that Marvell was superior to Parker even in wit." He forgets what Swift says: "We still read Marvell's answer to Parker with pleasure, though the book it answers is sunk long ago." See Swift's Apology for the Tale of a Tub.

shaken;" he swaggered about the streets of London in cassock and gown, and was "so lifted up with pride that he was insufferable to all that came near him." No writer of the day equalled in profanity, scurrillity, and buffoonery, the Archbishop's chaplain. Nonconformists he calls, villains,—hypocrites,—sons of Belial,—rebels,—schismatics,—greatest heretics,—old boyes to be lashed out of their peevishness. Dr. John Owen, the honoured chief of the Independents, he calls "the great bell-wether of disturbance and sedition—a viper, so swollen with venom, that it must either burst or spit its poison." Tender consciences must be restrained with more peremptory and unyielding rigour, than naked and unsanctified villany,—peevish principles about religion must be suppressed more than the foulest crimes of immorality,—princes may with less hazard give liberty to men's vices and debaucheries than to their consciences,—there is little difference between a *tender* conscience and a *soft* head,—weakness of conscience proceeds from want of wit. These six lines he recommended as more useful than all the Puritan sermons:

> By the Liturgy, daily pray,
> So pray and praise God every day;
> The Apostles' Creed, believe also,
> Do as you would be done unto;
> Receive the Sacrament as well as you can,
> This is the whole duty of man.

One of his profane sayings was, "The king was indeed under God, yet he was not under Christ, but above Him." Hooker is a name reverenced by most churchmen; Parker calls him "a long-winded old fellow." He thought little of prayers or any exercises of devotion, which he seldom attended, for "as to religion he was rather impious." Such was the man honoured by Sheldon's friendship, created his chaplain, Archdeacon of Canterbury, Prebendary of Canterbury, Rector of Ickham, and Rector of Chartham.*

* Sheldon "honoured him, not only by patronage, but with friendship." Carwithen's Hist. vol. ii. p. 494. Baxter, part iii. pp. 41, 42, 106, 141. Athenæ Oxon. Parker. Burnet, vol. i. p. 541; vol. iii. p. 137. Life of Dr. John Owen, p. 89. Calamy's Baxter, p. 590. D'Oyly's Life of Sancroft, vol. i. p. 237. For a full account of this degraded man's life and writings, see " The Rehearsal Transprosed." For other specimens of Sheldon's chaplains, see Baxter, part ii. p. 374. Noble's continuation of Granger, vol. iii. p. 76. Dove's Life of Marvell, p. 39.

CHAPTER V.

JAMES II. ENDEAVOURS TO INTRODUCE POPERY.—CHURCHMEN AND DISSENTERS COALESCE.—SANCROFT'S SCHEME FOR REVISING THE PRAYER BOOK AND RESTORING DISSENTERS.—THE REVOLUTION.—LORD NOTTINGHAM'S COMPREHENSION BILL.—FACTIOUS CONDUCT OF THE HIGH CHURCH CLERGY.—THE LIBERAL CLERGY PROMOTED.—THE LAST ATTEMPT TO RESTORE DISSENTERS DEFEATED BY CONVOCATION.—SACHEVERELL.—CONCLUSION.

WHEN James II. ascended the throne, gloomy was the state of the nation; almost every living soul cried at the death of Charles, not so much from sorrow for him as from dread of James.* The Whigs were vanquished; the dissenters crushed; Lord William Russell and Algernon Sidney had been slain; no Hampden dared to raise his voice in defence of the rights of the subject; the nation was couching down like a broken-spirited beast, ready to receive any burden which its Royal master chose to lay upon it. The Tories were pleased with their new king, whom they could trust more than his fickle brother.† The pulpits of the church were ringing with the senseless doctrines of passive obedience, non-resistance, the divine right of an hereditary monarch. Sancroft had succeeded Sheldon; he was a pious, conscientious man, but timid, irresolute, and retiring. The Duke of York had put him forward against Compton, Bishop of London, thinking him less likely to interfere with the design of introducing Popery.‡ "The dissenters expected not only greater severities and rigours than before, but concluded they should, if it were possible, be extirpated."

---

* Lives of the Norths, vol. ii. p. 109. Thoresby's Diary, vol. i. p. 80.
† Thoresby's Correspondence, vol. i. pp. 54, 80. Fox's Hist., p. 77. Lives of the Norths, vol. ii. pp. 109, 116-121; vol. iii. p. 157. North's Examen, p. 647.
‡ Anthony à Wood's Life, Dec. 29th, 1677. Welwood's Memoirs. Lives of the Norths, vol. ii. p. 127.

The king, in his first speech to the Privy Council, promised to defend and support the church of England. The declaration was received with extravagant joy. Sancroft, with some of the bishops, threw themselves at his majesty's feet, and thanked him for his "admirable declaration, which we ought to write down in letters of gold, and engrave on marble."* The Universities hastened to assure the king, that they would obey him "without limitations or restrictions." An eminent London clergyman, Dr. Sharp, exclaimed in his pulpit, "as to our religion, we have the word of the king, which (with reverence be it spoken) is as sacred as my text." The common phrase was, "We have now the word of a king, and a word never yet broken." Not only the clergy, but large numbers of church laymen were infected with slavish principles, and would have concurred in establishing arbitrary government under a Protestant sovereign.† But fortunately for this country, James II. was a member of the church of Rome, and too zealous a

* The Appendix to Clarendon's Correspondence, vol. ii. p. 472. As the king advanced in his progress towards arbitrary power, some of the clergy became more servile. Cartwright, Dean of Ripon, preaching on Feb. 6th, 1685, taught the people that no one should resist or question the king. "Who questioned Saul for slaying the priests, and revolting to idolatry? The king may make use of this prerogative, as God does of His Omnipotence upon some extraordinary occasion." In another sermon, he says: "The king's promises are free donatives, and ought not to be too strictly examined or urged; and that they must leave his majesty to explain his own meaning in them." The king was so delighted with this audacious assertion, that he made him Bishop of Chester.
On May 12th, 1685, Sherlock preached before the Commons on "The Divine right of kingly government." In the same year, the Dean of Bristol told his congregation that they must obey the king without any limit, and suffer patiently oppression, "King James shall be known in the ages to come by this appellative of King James the Just, the Prince of his Word." In the same year, Pelling preached a similar sermon in Westminster Abbey The preacher at the Chapel Royal said, "the Church teacheth subjection and loyalty *without any reserve.*"

† Hallam, vol. ii. p. 411. Rapin, vol. ii. p. 741. Burnet, vol. iii. p. 7. Neal, vol. v. p. 2. Kennet, vol. iii. p. 441. Correspondence of Pepys, vol. ii. p. 65. Sharp's Life, vol. i. p. 64. Dalrymple's Memoirs, vol. i. pp. 109-112.

member to allow the Anglican church to remain undisturbed. He broke with the church; that led to his own ruin and England's deliverance. When the rebellion of Monmouth was crushed, James soon discovered his design of introducing Popery, as well as arbitrary power. Great was the perplexity of the men who had been insisting on the senseless plea of a Divine right.* They now found that he who would be the king's friend, must be the church's enemy. The Tories were too firmly attached to Protestantism to aid James in restoring Popery. James cast off his old friends and thought that he could destroy the religious as well as the civil liberties of the people; he persuaded himself that the days of the Anglican church were numbered. When the daughter of Waller the poet was about to be married to a clergyman, the king sent a message to him, "that he wondered he could have any thoughts of marrying his daughter to a falling church." Waller made answer, "Sir, the king does me very great honour to take any notice of my domestic affairs; but I have lived long enough to observe that this *falling* church has got a trick of *rising* again."†

Encouraged by the king, the Jesuits and priests became uncommonly bold and active. Romish books and pamphlets against the church were sold on every stall, cried about by hawkers in the streets, thrown into houses, sent by penny post bundles over the kingdom, brought into coffee houses. The priests of the foreign ministers catechized English children, tampered with dying persons, argued in hackney coaches, baptized children against the parents' wish.‡

Alarmed at James's attacks upon the church, the London

---

* Welwood's Memoirs, pp. 150, 151. Fox's Hist. p. 39. Allibon's charge in Gutch's Collection. Dalrymple's Memoirs, vol. i. p. 159.
† Waller's Life, p. 38.
‡ Gutch's Collection, vol. i. No. 43.

divines preached with boldness against the errors of Rome. Now did the men who had been reviled and sneered at as trimmers—the church's treacherous undermining friends—your liberal clergy—sons of latitude—broadway clergy,—stand forth, and gain immortal honours by their courage and learning and eloquence. Tillotson, Stillingfleet, Tenison, Patrick, Wake, Whitby, Sharp, Williams, Burnet, Fowler, with Atterbury, Sherlock, Aldrich, and others, battled with Rome, and drove her defenders from the field. The pious Bishop Ken distinguished himself by his eloquent sermons against Popery, and people crowded from all quarters to hear him.* The king was angry with the church of England men, upon whom he had boasted he could depend; and too well had they supported him and his brother in their sanguinary measures. When Burnet once told him, that he being a Papist could not reign in quiet, he quickly answered, "Does not the church of England maintain the doctrine of non-resistance and passive obedience."† Compton, bishop of London, won immense applause by his spirited conduct; he was called the Protestant Bishop. The king discoursing with him on some tender subjects, was so much displeased with his answers that he said, "He talked more like a colonel than a divine." Compton had been in the army, and replied, "His majesty did him honour in taking notice of his having formerly drawn his sword in defence of the constitution, and that he should do the same again if he lived to see it necessary."‡

* Evelyn's Diary, March 10th, 20th; April 1st, 1687. Baxter, part iii. p. 85. Nicholls's Literary Anecdotes, vol. i. p. 394. Dryden's Hind and Panther, part iii.

† Speech of Burnet at Sacheverell's Trial. State Trials. Lives of the Norths, vol. i. p. 313; vol. iii. pp. 268-270. See James's First Speech to his Privy Council.

‡ Ellis's Original Letters, vol. iv. p. 84. Granger's Biog. Hist.

The enraged priests of Rome advised the king to prohibit the clergy from preaching on controversial subjects. Silenced in their pulpits, the church of England heroes betake themselves to the press. Every week some able tract against Rome appeared from the pens of these masters of the English language; the nation was astonished at the superiority of the Anglican clergy. A gentleman writing to his friend says, "The bishop of London's fame runs high in the vogue of the people, the London pulpits ring strong peals against Popery; and I have lately heard there never were such eminently able men to serve in those cures."*

There was now open war between the king and the church. It was therefore determined that the dissenters should be gained to support the king's designs. The judges were instructed to revile the church; she was held up as a cruel and bloody church. The cruelties which the clergy had committed upon the Nonconformists, was a common topic of conversation with the king. He discoursed admirably to the Oxford men, told them to live in love and charity, to put away pride, be humble, charitable, and love one another. Dissenters were encouraged to tell of the persecutions they had endured.† Philip Henry among others was asked to give an account of his sufferings; he said, all the country knew how his goods had been carried away, but to give any particular account he declined, having "long since, from his heart,

---

* Welwood's Memoirs, p. 174. Ellis's Letters, vol. iv. p. 84. Burnet, vol. iii. pp. 98, 99. Evelyn's Diary, March 7th & 14th, June 20th, 1686, March 10th and 20th, 1687, April 1st, 1687. Neal, vol. v. p. 14. Kennet's Hist. vol. iii. p. 452. Sharp's Life, vol. i. pp. 48, 49.

† For references to the sufferings endured by dissenters, see Thoresby's Diary. Dec. 31st, 1681; Jan. 1st, May 13th, July 4th and 5th, July 9th, Aug. 6th, Oct. 31st, 1682; Feb. 10th, Oct. 6th, 1683.

forgiven all the agents, instruments, and occasions of it ; and having purposed never to say anything more of it."*

The king's next step was to issue " a declaration for liberty of conscience," by which the penal laws in matters ecclesiastical were immediately suspended, and all men allowed " to meet and serve God after their own way and manner." (April 4th, 1687.) Many dissenters were caught by the bait, and presented addresses of thanks to the king in the same fulsome terms that had been used by churchmen. " The indulgence gave us ease," writes a Nonconformist, " though we dreaded a snake in the grass."† Five bishops were so base as to persuade their clergy to thank the king for promising to protect the established church. Dr. Samuel Parker, Sheldon's profane chaplain, who had been made Bishop of Oxford by James, and now preparing to turn Papist as Popery was in power, tried to induce his clergy to do the same, but without success, for not one would sign. Baxter was liberated from the prison where he had been lying for two years. Howe returned from Holland ; but before he left, the sagacious Prince of Orange warned him of the king's design, and implored him to urge upon the dissenters to be very sparing of their " congratulatory addresses."‡ There was a meeting of the London dissenting ministers to consider the course they should take. Howe declared against the power which the king claimed of suspending laws : Dr. Daniel Williams said,

---

* See the account of James's visit to Oxford, in Anthony à Wood's Life. Life of Philip Henry, p. 191. Letters from Dr. Sykes to Dr. Charlett, Sept. 7th and Sept. 9th, 1687. Judge Allibon's Charge ; paper No. 61, and p. 304 in vol. i. Gutch's Collection.

† Thoresby's Diary, vol. i. p. 186. Echard's Hist. p. 1085. Kennet's Hist. vol. iii. p. 489. Evelyn's Diary, June 16th, 1687. Burnet, vol. iii. p. 174.

‡ Welwood's Memoirs, p. 180. Ellis's Letters, vol. iv. p. 98. Original Letters, Dr. Sykes to Dr. Charlett, Nov. 16th, 1687. Echard's Hist. p. 1086. Kennet's Hist. vol. iii. p. 490, note c. Life of Howe, p. 346.

he would rather lose his liberty, and return to his former bondage, than give up the constitution and support the king's claim to set aside the laws of the land: the meeting was generally of the like opinion. There was at the same time a meeting of the city clergy, waiting to know the result. Howe made known the views of his brethren; the court was displeased, and the clergy encouraged by their patriotism.* An ejected minister was known to have kept a list of those Nonconformists who had suffered since the Restoration. The niggardly king—who would wear an old coarse French hat edged with a little bit of lace not worth a groat—offered a thousand guineas for the manuscript; the generous dissenter declined the offer, he would not blacken the church to promote Popery.

The clergy began to open their eyes and repent of their folly in keeping out of the church and persecuting Nonconformists. Some, says Welwood, who had been zealous in persecuting dissenters, now saw their error too late, and found they had been used as tools by the Romish party to prevent the dissenters uniting with the church. The dissenters were convinced that the design of the king was to destroy the church first, and them afterwards. Churchmen and dissenters drew nearer and nearer as the danger increased. A few violent dissenters continued to support the king, but they had no influence; they were ridiculed as "the Pope's journeymen." It was a comical sight to see Lobb the Presbyterian, and Father Petre the Jesuit, as great intimates as if they were of the same society. To prevent the dissenters joining the court, a letter, which had been approved by some eminent dignitaries in the church, was published and dispersed throughout the kingdom. No name was attached to it, but it was

* Life of Howe, p. 348. Neal, vol. v. p. 37.

known to be from the pen of one of the most accomplished statesmen of the day—the Marquis of Halifax. It thus warns the dissenters against their new friends :—Rome does not only dislike your liberty, but by its principles cannot allow it. You are therefore hugged now, only that you may be the better squeezed another time; the other day you were the sons of Belial, now you are angels of light. Take warning by the mistake of the church of England, when after the Restoration they preserved so long the bitter taste of your rough usage to them, that it made them forget their interest, and sacrifice it to their revenge. If it be said the church is only humble when it is out of power, the answer is, that is uncharitable, and an unseasonable triumph; if the church would comply with the court, she could turn all the thunder upon yourselves, and blow you off the stage with a breath. The church is now convinced of its error,—the bishops are no longer rigid prelates,—all former haughtiness towards you is for ever extinguished, and the spirit of persecution is turned into a spirit of peace, charity, and condescension; there is a general agreement of thinking men, that we must no more cut ourselves off from foreign Protestants, *but enlarge our foundations.**

So runs this masterly letter; the dissenters were satisfied, determined to stand or fall with the church.

The gloomy bigot rushes on to his ruin; the hour of England's deliverance from Stuart tyranny draws near. On May 4th, 1688, the king published an order that his illegal declaration of liberty of conscience should be read by the clergy in time of divine service. The clergy were amazed; if they read the declaration the church was lost; if they refused, they would be cast out of their livings. They must either eat their own words, and give up the divine right, which they had been

* Welwood's Memoirs, pp. 168, 169. Parl. Hist. Appendix, vol. iv.

senselessly proclaiming; or betray the church, as some of them had the constitution.* The bishops generously interposed, and took upon themselves the responsibility, by refusing to send the declaration to their clergy. Archbishop Sancroft hastily summoned some of the bishops and leading London divines to meet at Lambeth. Amongst other arguments in favour of reading the declaration, it was said, Dissenters would think that the clergy refused to read it from an unwillingness to shew tenderness towards them. It was answered, "Dissenters had never such assurances from churchmen of their inclination of tenderness to them, as they then received."† In the famous petition of the seven bishops to the king, they declared that their unwillingness to publish the declaration was not "from any want of tenderness to dissenters, in relation to whom we are willing to come to such a temper as shall be thought fit, when the matter shall be considered and settled in Parliament and Convocation." Some sneered at the fine promises of the bishops; it was said: "They promise to come to a temper, but it is only such an one as they themselves should settle in Convocation." Churchmen denied this; one confidently declared that the bishops will perform all their promises, and that they will firmly carry out *their moderate resolutions, and not yield to the passions of any of the inferior clergy.* "I will boldly say, that if the church of England, after she has got out of this storm, will return to hearken to the peevishness of some sour men, she will be abandoned both of God and man, and will set heaven and earth against her." The Bishop of St. Asaph, passing through Oswestry, sent for the Independent minister: "You and we," he said, "are brethren; we have indeed been angry brethren, but we have seen our folly, and are resolved, if ever we have it in our

* See a firm letter from a clergyman to Pepys, refusing to read the declaration. Pepys's Life, vol. ii., p. 125. † Echard's History, p. 1101.

power, to shew that we will treat you as brethren." Four days before the trial of the seven bishops, one of them told young Henry Wharton, "if himself and his brethren should escape the present rage of the Papists, they were resolved to use their utmost endeavours to purge the church from all corruptions; to procure the admission of the sober and pious dissenters into the church, a thing so much wished for."*

The clergy, before the acquittal of the seven bishops, were expecting to be ruined. Howe was dining with Dr. Sherlock, then Master of the Temple ; the conversation was on the imminent danger with which the church was threatened. Suddenly Sherlock asked Howe, what he thought the dissenters would do, should the livings of the church become vacant, and be offered to them. Howe thought that the doctor's fears would not be realised; but Sherlock said, the bishops now imprisoned in the tower will certainly be cast ; the rest of the clergy who had so generally refused to read the declaration would be deprived of their livings, which must be offered to Nonconformists, "and who knows," he concluded, " but Mr. Howe may be offered the place of Master of the Temple." Howe replied at some length; if the place were offered him, he might not decline altogether such an opportunity of usefulness, if it were offered on such terms as he could conscientiously accept, *but as for the emolument, he should have nothing to do with it, except to convey it to its legal owner.* Sherlock was delighted, rose from his chair, embraced him, and told him "how rejoiced he was to find him that ingenuous, honest man he had always supposed him to be."†

---

* D'Oyly's Life of Sancroft, vol. ii. p. 134.

† Howe related this occurrence to a dignitary of the church, to whom Sherlock was well known. "Sir," replied the dignitary, "you must give me leave to say, that if you had studied the case for seven years together, you could not have said anything which had been more to the purpose, or more to Dr. Sherlock's satisfaction." Life of Howe, pp. 350, 351. Welwood's Memoirs, p. 183.

On June 30th, 1688, the bishops were acquitted; "bonfires were made that night, and bells rung," for the triumph of the church was felt to be the triumph of the nation. When the bishops waited upon the king after their acquittal, people were suspicious, and feared that they might be drawn into compliances with the king. To allay these groundless fears, an account of their interview with his majesty was written by Dr. Sherlock, concluding with these words: "I do assure you, and I am certain I have the best grounds in the world for my assurance, that the bishops will never stir one jot from their petition; but that they will, whenever that happy opportunity shall offer itself, let the Protestant dissenters find that they will be better than their word given in their famous petition."* It was often said, "If ever God should deliver us out of our present distress, we would keep up our domestic quarrels no more." The dissenters acknowledged the firm and dignified stand which the London divines had made against Rome. They confessed that they had wronged the bishops in accusing them of being inclined to Popish principles. Even the Scotch Presbyterians revered them. There was every prospect now of a re-union of churchmen and Puritans, and it was pretty generally agreed, that the ceremonies which had been the cause of so much mischief, should no longer be forced upon those who objected to them.† It was visible to all the nation, says Wake, Bishop of Lincoln, that the more moderate dissenters were generally so well satisfied with that stand which our divines had made against Popery, and the many unanswerable treatises they had published in confutation of it, as to express an unusual readiness to come

* Sherlock's account of the proposals of the bishops to the king. Kennet's History, vol. iii. p. 521, note d.
† Echard's Hist., p. 1107. D'Oyly's Life of Sancroft, vol. i. p. 325. Rapin's Hist., vol. ii. pp. 755, 758, 770. Sir G. Mackenzie's letter to Sancroft, in Gutch's Collection. Ellis's Letters, 2nd series, pp. 108, 109.

into us.* The primate was touched by the patriotism of the dissenters. He calls them his Protestant brethren, differing from us in lesser matters, but holding with us the substance of Reformed Christianity—children of the same father, who should join and assist one another, and be united, if we cannot in fellowship, in Christian affection and charity. His articles of advice to the clergy (July 16th, 1688) breathe a charitable spirit. In the letter which accompanied the articles the attention of the clergy is called to the zeal the Archbishop expresses against Rome on the one hand, "and the unhappy differences that are among Protestants on the other." In the eleventh of these articles, the clergy are exhorted to " have a very tender regard to our brethren, the Protestant dissenters,"—to visit them, receive them kindly,—treat them fairly,—discourse with them calmly and civilly,—to persuade them (if it may be) to a full compliance with the church,—to convince them that the bishops are irreconcilable enemies to Rome,—to affectionately exhort them to prayer, for the blessed universal union of all reformed churches both at home and abroad against common enemies, that all they who confess the name of the Lord "may meet in one holy communion, and live in perfect unity and godly love."† Thus was the persecuting policy which had prevailed from the Restoration repudiated; the forcing, chastising, lashing, scourging system, had for a time no defender. The principles of the the liberals were triumphant; the Act of Uniformity was emphatically condemned.

The bishops were now resolved to repair the mischief of Black Bartholomew's Day. The Archbishop and clergy of

---

* Wake's Speech at Sacheverell's Trial.

† See a remarkable paper of Sancroft's, draught of answer to the four titular bishops, in Gutch's Collection, vol. i., and another paper in p. 266. Echard's Hist. p. 1107. D'Oyly's Life of Sancroft, vol. ii. pp. 319, 324, 325.

London had several conferences with the chief of the dissenting ministers. Sancroft at once proceeded to draw out a scheme, by which the moderate dissenters might be taken into the church of England. He was convinced that there had been a sad mistake made at the Restoration, and foreseeing that some great political change was drawing near, he was resolved that another such happy opportunity of perfecting the Prayer Book, and strengthening the church by gaining dissenters, should not be lost. The Archbishop took one part of the scheme; to Dr. Patrick he committed another; the revision of the Prayer Book he referred to Dr. Sharp, Dr. Moore, and a select number of divines. The design was this: to amend the discipline of the church, to review and enlarge the Liturgy, and to propose to Convocation and Parliament, that those ceremonies which were allowed to be indifferent should not be forced upon those who had prejudices against them.*

But whilst this excellent scheme was being worked out, important political events occurred which prevented the Archbishop bringing it to a completion. The nation could no longer bear with the misrule of James II. To Holland men looked for deliverance; earnest invitations were sent to William, Prince of Orange, to interfere and preserve our liberties and religion. On Nov. 5th, 1688, the Prince landed in England. In the next month, James fled, and we were delivered from a race whose rule had been one continued invasion of our rights and liberties. Englishmen were not to be slaves to princes or priests. The Lords and Commons

* The only account of Sancroft's scheme is that given by Dr. William Wake, when Bishop of Lincoln, in his speech in the House of Lords, at the trial of Dr. Sacheverell, March 17th, 1710. There is mention of it in "A letter from a divine to a member of Parliament, in defence of the bill for uniting Protestants," licensed April 1st, 1689. This is the treatise to which Wake refers in his speech. Kennet's Hist. vol. iii. p. 588, note *a.* D'Oyly's Life of Sancroft, vol. i. p. 326. Hallam, vol. iii. p. 172. Echard's Hist. p. 1107. Ellis's Letters, vol. iv. p. 117.

invited the Prince of Orange to take upon himself the administration of affairs, and thanked him for coming to rescue this nation "from the miseries of popery and slavery." On Ash-Wednesday (Feb. 13th), 1689, the crown was tendered to the Prince and Princess of Orange, and on the same day they were proclaimed King William III. and Queen Mary.

There was again "a glorious opportunity of reconciling all moderate dissenters to the communion of the church of England, which might have been happily effected if this extraordinary juncture had been well-managed and improved." William had already promised, with the concurrence and at the request of the leading churchmen, to "use his endeavours to bring about the so much desired union between the church of England and the dissenters." The dissenters publicly expressed their wish for union with the church. A large number of them waited upon the king, and presented to him an address, in which they express their desire and hope, that the king will use his authority to establish a firm union between Protestants in matters of religion. The king replied, "Whatever is in my power shall be employed for obtaining such an union among you." Still more strongly did they express the same wish in their speech to the queen, in which they said, "We humbly desire your majesty will be pleased by your wisdom and goodness, to compose the differences between your Protestant subjects, in things of less moment concerning religion. We hope those reverend persons who conspire with us in the main end, the glory of God, and the public good, will consent to the terms of union, wherein all the reformed churches agree." The queen replied, "I will use all endeavours for the obtaining an union that is necessary for the edifying of the church." Their majesties were in favour of Sancroft's scheme, and "openly espoused the design:" the most eminent clergy had pledged themselves to accomplish it, but they were again to be thwarted by men who boasted themselves to be the church's friends, and have ever been her worst enemies.*

The part which Sancroft played at the Revolution was not a glorious one. His conduct in the hour of the church's great peril was heroic, and if there had been need, he would have willingly shed his blood in her defence. He was a good, but not a great man, and could not free himself from those unconstitutional principles which held in bondage so many churchmen. Since the flight of James, he seemed to be in a maze. His friends pressed him to wait upon the Prince of Orange, or send some message to him, " but he was positive not to do it." Lord Clarendon, son of the great Lord Clarendon, and the bishops, urged him to attend the meeting of the Lords, but he steadily refused; he would do nothing, say nothing. On January 3rd, 1689, Lord Clarendon and Dr. Tenison were dining at Lambeth. They spoke to him of the approaching meeting of the Lords and Commons, and asked him "whether he would not think of preparing something against that time in behalf of the dissenters." Dr. Tenison added, it would be expected that something should be offered in fulfilment of the declaration made in the petition of the seven bishops. The archbishop said, "he knew well what was in their petition; and he believed every bishop in England intended to make it good when there was an opportunity of debating those matters in Convocation; but till then, or without a commission from the king, it was highly penal to enter upon church matters; but, however, he would have it in his mind, and would be willing to discourse with any of the bishops or clergy thereupon, if they came to him;

* Kennet's Hist. vol. iii. p. 558.   Calamy's Baxter, p. 636.   Wake's Speech in the House of Lords, at Sacheverell's Trial.

though he believed the dissenters would never agree among themselves with what concessions they would be satisfied." Dr. Tenison replied, "he thought so too, but the way to do good was, for the bishops to endeavour *to get such concessions settled in Parliament, which, whether accepted by the dissenters or not, would be good for the church.*" The archbishop answered, "that when there was a Convocation, those matters would be considered of; and in the meantime he knew not what to say, but that he would think of what had been offered by us."* It appears from this conversation, which is characteristic of Sancroft's timorous disposition,† that he had not yet come to a decision on that part of his scheme which related to the concessions to be made to dissenters; but Dr. Tenison's sound advice was not without effect, for a few days after, there was a meeting of some of the leading churchmen, to consult about such concessions as might bring in dissenters. There were present, the Bishop of St. Asaph, Stillingfleet, Tillotson, Tenison, Patrick, and Sharp; these two last-named divines were employed by Sancroft in drawing out the scheme of comprehension, and probably the others were also. The Bishop of St. Asaph stated, that they had the archbishop's leave to proceed; the result was, says Patrick, "We agreed that a bill should be prepared to be offered to Parliament by the bishops." The bill was drawn out in ten or eleven heads.‡ As Sancroft had resolved not to take the oaths to the new sovereigns, and persevered in his refusal to attend the House of Lords, the Comprehension Bill and Toleration Bill were moved for by some of the bishops, and offered to the House of Lords by the Earl of Nottingham. This nobleman was a

---

* Diary of Henry, Earl of Clarendon, Jan. 3rd, 1689.
† Another instance of his timid disposition is mentioned by Evelyn in his Diary, May 12th, 1686.
‡ Autobiography of Patrick, Jan. 14th, 1688.

Tory, a High Churchman,* and one of the few statesmen who served King William honestly. The title of the bill is, "An Act for the uniting of their majesties' Protestant subjects;"† it passed the Lords after some alterations, and was sent to the Commons. There it met with a treatment which astonished and mortified its promoters, for it was not only opposed by the men who had driven the Puritans out of the church, and resisted every attempt to restore them; it was neglected by those who where favourable to the dissenters. These Whigs reasoned in this manner: If this bill passes, two-thirds of the dissenting ministers will enter the church. In becoming churchmen they will become probably Tories, and thus we shall lose a large body of our supporters; further, the church will become so strong, and dissent so weak, that the Toleration Act will be endangered.‡ Had the Whigs been united, the bill would have been carried, for the extreme Tory party were a minority in the House. Lord Nottingham's friends seeing that by this coalition the bill would be defeated, availed themselves of the suggestion that the bill should lie on the table until the clergy had an opportunity of declaring their opinions. "The proposition was received with general acclamation. The Tories were well pleased to see such honour done to the priesthood.

* The term High Church was not yet in common use. South, in 1698, complains of those who are for strict conformity to the rules of the church, being called " of late," High Churchmen, and those of the contrary way are " sanctified by the fashionable, endearing name of Low Churchmen, not from their affecting a lower condition in the church than others, since none lie so low but they can look as high: but from the low condition which the authors of this distinction would fain bring the church itself into."—Epistle Dedicatory to the Archbishop of Dublin.

† The bill is fully described by Lord Macaulay; he examined the only copy in existence, which, he observes "has been seen by only two or three persons now living." It is in the archives of the House of Lords. Macaulay's Hist. vol. iv. p. 93.

‡ Such seem to me to have been their motives. Bogue and Bennett's Hist. of Dissenters, vol. i. p. 217. See Speaker Onslow's note on Burnet's account of this matter. Macaulay's Hist. vol. iv. p. 100.

Those Whigs who were against the Comprehension Bill were well pleased to see it laid aside, certainly for a year, probably for ever. Those Whigs who were for the Comprehension Bill were well pleased to escape without a defeat." The Lords and Commons addressed the king, praying him to summon the Convocation; and Lord Nottingham's Comprehension Bill was not again mentioned.* The Toleration Act, the Magna Charta of religious liberty, received the royal assent, May 24th, 1689.

Whilst the Comprehension Bill was before Parliament, Tillotson, who had great influence with the king, "who used to call him the honestest man and the best friend that ever he had in his life," advised William to try another method for accomplishing the object. He reminded him that the Papists reproached the church of England with being founded on Parliamentary authority, and therefore recommended that his majesty should grant a royal commission, consisting of the most eminent clergy, to consider of some methods for healing the church's wounds, and establishing a durable peace; the recommendations of these commissioners, he advised, should be laid before Convocation and Parliament. Upon this advice the king acted; ten bishops and twenty eminent divines were authorised to revise the Liturgy, and consider some other ecclesiastical matters. Tillotson was one of the most amiable of men, and he thought that the clergy would, after their recent danger, be more kindly disposed towards dissenters, and be willing to fulfil the promises which had been made when the church was struggling with Rome. Never was any one more mistaken. Burnet, as soon as he heard that the Convocation were to be

---

* Whilst this bill was passing the Lords, Locke wrote to Limborch, March 12th, 1689, saying the "clergy were no great friends to it." See his Familiar Letters to his Friends, at the end of vol. iii. of his Works, 1722. Macaulay's Hist. vol. iv. p. 116. Birch's Life of Tillotson, p. 163. Calamy's Baxter, p. 654. Burnet, vol. iv. p. 17-21. Hallam, vol. iii. p. 173.

summoned, said to Lord Halifax, in his blunt way, "it would be the utter ruin of the Comprehension scheme." Lord Halifax agreed with him, for he knew the church people would never receive the Presbyterians among them. Burnet and Halifax were right. As the fear of Popery passed away, the old rancorous evil spirit returned; and the disciples of Sheldon again made themselves heard. Every day the outcry against altering the Liturgy, and admitting dissenters into the church became louder. The Universities took fire: the angry men of Oxford again calumniated the moderate churchmen as Latitudinarians, Socinians: the parochial clergy followed in the same strain. They said,—the church is going to be ruined, undermined, subverted,—if alterations are commenced, no one can tell where they will stop,—frequent changes would make people lose their esteem for the Prayer Book,—making concessions would be a confession that the church had been hitherto in the wrong,—better to have a schism without the church, than a faction within it,—the oaths, subscriptions, and ceremonies were imposed only to keep out the Puritans, we will never consent to their removal to let them in again,—the six hundred alterations made at the Restoration were rejected with scorn, and had no effect, we cannot expect such persons to be satisfied,*— dissenters were now tolerated, they should be content,—they

* It is scarcely necessary to point out the contradiction between this assertion, and the admission that at the Restoration new terms were imposed for the purpose of driving out the Puritans. The truth is, no concessions have been made to the Puritan portion of the church since 1552. Neal may be allowed to speak for the Puritans; of Elizabeth's alterations in 1559, he says, "no alterations were made in favour of those who now began to be called Puritans;" again, he says of her Prayer Book, "it was hardly equal to that which was set out by King Edward VI." in 1552. The few changes made by James I. in 1604, "were (to use the present learned Bishop of Llandaff's words) certainly not calculated to place the Puritan or low church party in more favourable circumstances." The changes in 1661 were, as has been said, undoubtedly anti-Puritan. All church legislation since the beginning of Elizabeth's reign has been adverse to the Puritans.

were not agreed among themselves as to what they wanted,—the king was a Presbyterian, and about to betray the church in England as he had done in Scotland,—the English Presbyterians would be as intolerant, if they got the upper hand, as their Scotch brethren, who were insulting and persecuting the Episcopal clergy in that country. Such were the cries raised by the men, who became known about this time, as High Churchmen.

There was, however, one objection, and only one, of considerable weight. It was said,—if extensive alterations are made in the Liturgy, the clergy who are intending to refuse the oaths to William and Mary, will pretend that they still stick to the ancient church of England, and to the old Prayer Book, in opposition to those who adopt the revised one. It is probable that the non-jurors would have set up this specious pretext for a schism. The simple and moderate bill of Lord Nottingham was not open to this objection ;* for it did not alter the Liturgy, but merely removed the mischievous declaration of assent and consent to the Prayer Book, required by the Act of Uniformity and made indifferent the ceremonies to which dissenters generally objected. The neglect which Lord Nottingham's bill received was the fatal mistake ; for it was evident from the cries now raised that the clergy would never consent to enlarge the church.

* It is said, that the non-jurors hoped that the Liturgy might be altered, that they might have an excuse for a schism ; yet Sancroft approved of Lord Nottingham's bill, which was moved for by the non-juring bishops. After the bill had passed the Lords, Sancroft gave no sign against it, as appears from the conversation between him, the bishop of St. Asaph, and Evelyn, in Evelyn's Diary, April 12th, 1689. Kennet's Hist. vol. iii. pp. 591, 799. Burnet, vol. iv. pp. 50, 52, 54, 57, 59. Calamy's Baxter, pp. 658, 659, 660. Birch's Life of Tillotson, pp. 164, 181, 183. The case of Protestant dissenters represented and argued, by John Howe, 1689. The non-jurors themselves soon altered the Liturgy ; even in 1690 a Liturgy drawn up for Jacobite families appeared. Kennet's Hist. p. 615, note b.

The commissioners appointed by King William to revise the Prayer Book were, with few exceptions, of the Latitudinarian school—the disciples of Selden, Falkland, Hales, Chillingworth and Jeremy Taylor, whose principles were now victorious. They were a body of divines, the honour and glory of their country, and now were raised to the high places of the church. The episcopal bench has never since or before been filled with so many liberal men. Tillotson was made Archbishop of Canterbury; Stillingfleet, Burnet, Patrick, Fowler, Sharp, Denison, Kidder, became bishops. Tillotson and Stillingfleet had been engaged in most of the unsuccessful attempts that had been made since the Restoration, to enlarge the communion of the church. There were many points of resemblance in the lives of these two great men. Tillotson was five years older than Stillingfleet: Cambridge had the honour of rearing them: they were ordained within a short time of each other: they were soon close friends, hiring the Mansion-house at Cheshunt, to live "there together in summer-time:" in 1672, Tillotson became Dean of Canterbury, five years afterwards, Stillingfleet Dean of St. Paul's: at the Revolution the former was raised to the Archbishopric of Canterbury, the latter to the Bishopric of Worcester: Tillotson died in 1694, five years afterwards, Stillingfleet followed. "They were lovely and pleasant in their lives, and in their death they were not divided."*

But all their labours were in vain. There was spreading through the clergy, an angry, discontented spirit. Within a month after James fled, they "began to change their note, both in pulpit and discourse, on their old passive obedience."† Although the clergy, except about four hundred, took the oaths

---

* Anthony à Wood's Life, p. 96. Thoresby's Diary. Sharp's Life, vol. i. p. 48. Tillotson's Life in Ecc. Biog. Preface of Baxter's Life.

† Evelyn's Diary, Jan. 29th, 1689.

of allegiance to William and Mary, the hearts of many of them were with James. They had no love for the deliverer whom the Almighty had raised up to rescue from destruction, our liberties and religion. The Revolution disgusted them: all the slavish principles which for years they had been preaching, were repudiated by the nation: they whispered sedition, " we have forty thousand men to bring King James back : " they were exasperated by the taunts of those who had not taken the oaths, who sneered at them as "a jolly pack of swearers." Thus the parochial clergy were not sorry of an opportunity of shewing their power by thwarting the wishes of the king, and returned men to Convocation whose only recommendation seems to have been, that they would oppose every proposal which the royal commissioners might make to them.*

Henry, Earl of Clarendon, with his brother, the Earl of Rochester, were men of great influence with the clergy : the latter, by interest and education, a favourer of the servile principles prevalent in the church. Being uncles to the queen, they expected high offices to be offered to them. In this they were disappointed, and now they were gratifying their revenge by using their influence to defeat the scheme. Clarendon at one time appears to have been not unfavourable to some measure for drawing into the church moderate dissenters, but he soon returned to his intolerant views, and is described by a writer of the day, as "a true son of the church of England, a lover of the regular clergy."† Cornbury, the seat of Lord Clarendon, lies at a convenient distance from Oxford, the head quarters of the opposition; he was frequently there, and had oppor-

---

* Lord Macaulay observes that there was only one man of any note as a scholar returned by the parochial clergy.

† Wood's Fasti, vol. iv. p. 229.

tunities of animating the clergy in their opposition to the scheme of comprehension.*

The Convocation met in November. The bishops and the moderate clergy, as well as the king, wished Tillotson to be chosen prolocutor, or speaker; he was proposed by Sharp; but the Lords Clarendon and Rochester had found a man in Oxford ready for their purpose, who was put forward in opposition to Tillotson, this was Dr. Jane. He was the chief promoter of the famous Oxford decree in 1683, "against certain damnable doctrines," which had hung in triumph in the Colleges and Halls of Oxford, and was soon after the Revolution privately removed. The intrigues of Clarendon and Rochester were successful; their disappointed ambition was gratified; Jane was elected by a majority of two to one; Tillotson, who even in September thought that the clergy would make concessions, was now undeceived.† Jane, on being presented to Compton, Bishop of London, made the customary speech in Latin, extolling the church of England as being perfect, and intimating that he and his brethren were unwilling to make any changes. Compton replied; he told them that they should show charity and indulgence to dissenters, as the bishops and clergy had promised in the time of King James, and exhorted them to unanimity and concord.‡

* From his conversation with the archbishop on Jan. 3rd, I conclude that he was favourable to the comprehension scheme. On March 11th, he makes this entry in his diary: "In the evening I went to see Lord Abingdon; my lord was much concerned for the church, and very angry at the bill of comprehension. The Bishop of St. Asaph went with me; he is deep in that comprehending project." On April 25th, Dr. Tenison was with him, "we had much discourse about the designed comprehension, which I wonder so good a man should be fond of." See also his diary, Jan. 14th, and Nov. 17th, 1689. Fox's Hist. p. 79. See Anthony à Wood's Life for instances of Clarendon's influence at Oxford.

† Birch gives a copy of a paper which Tillotson sent to Lord Portland: it is called, "Concessions which will probably be made by the church of England for the union of Protestants; which I sent to the Earl of Portland by Dr. Stillingfleet, Sept. 13th, 1689." Sharp's Life, vol. i. p. 106. Baxter, part iii. p. 177.   ‡ Kennet's Hist. vol. iii. p. 591.

From the beginning to the end, "they displayed in everything a factious temper, which held the very names of concession and conciliation in abhorrence."* The bishops wished in their address to the king, to acknowledge the "great deliverance Almighty God wrought for us, by your means, in making you the blessed instrument of preserving us from falling under the cruelty of Popish tyranny." To their shame be it said, that the clergy refused to thank King William for the hazard he had run, in coming to rescue us from slavery.† Nothing that the bishops did pleased them; they treated the Bishop of London with indignity; they would listen to no arguments; dead to honour, they basely refused to fulfil the promises which had been made, when the fear of Popery was at its height; and succeeded by contemptible tactics, not omitting falsehood,‡ in defeating this last attempt to revise the Prayer Book, and enlarge the basis of the national church.

There was a bad spirit abroad in the church, ambitious, factious, intolerant, calumnious.§ Good men were grieved to see it. Archbishop Sharp spoke of the failure of the comprehension

* The railing at dissenters was soon resumed by the high church clergy. Thoresby's Correspondence, July 26th, 1694. Hallam, vol. iii. p. 173.

† Compare the address proposed by the bishops, with that presented to the king; the latter is, as Lord Macaulay calls it, cold, hard, and ungracious. Kennet's Hist., vol. iii. p. 593. Birch's Life of Tillotson, p. 188. Burnet, vol. iv. p. 57. Harleian Miscellany, p. 492. Burnet's Speech at Sacheverell's trial.

‡ Bishop Patrick says in his Autobiography: "They said their Speaker was not come, which afterwards we found to be false. We gave up several things rather than contend with them any longer." Thoresby's Diary, vol. i. p. 408.

§ The bitter, angry spirit of the opponents to alterations in the Liturgy and "the inviting of dissenters," may be understood by the following specimen of theological bitterness, from the pen of a leading man amongst them, (the Rev. Thomas Long,) who wrote warmly against the scheme. It is an Epitaph on Richard Baxter, "Here lies Richard Baxter, a militant divine, a reformed Jesuit, a brazen heresiarch, and the chief of schismatics, whose itch of disputing begat, whose humour of writing nourished, and whose intemperate zeal in preaching brought to its utmost height, the leprosy of the church; who dissented from those with whom he most agreed—from himself, as well as all other Nonconformists, past, present, and to come; the sworn

scheme with deep concern. Bishop Patrick "was concerned to find so little of a spirit of unity and concord." He was weary of the contention, and said with David, "O that I had wings like a dove, for then I would flee away, and be at rest." "For the divisions of Reuben, there were great searchings of heart."* Tillotson, full of that charity which hopeth all things, did not yet despair; writing to Frederick Spanheim, (Feb. 6th, 1691,) he says,—Stillingfleet and very many others, the glories and ornaments of our church, have strong inclinations to peace and concord; a union between the church and dissenters should not be attempted at present, but we ought to wait till the times grow more disposed for peace, a period which, I presage, is not far distant.† Bates had done all he could to promote a "comprehension as long as there was any hope, but at last, he saw there was none, till God should give a more suitable spirit to all concerned." Howe, himself calm amidst the fierce strife of tongues, spoke words of peace and love; he put forth "Humble requests both to Conformists and Dissenters," persuading both to charity, and "bend towards one common course, that there may at length cease to be any divided parties at all." There are, he says, different tastes in meats and drinks, we need not then wonder that men have different tastes in the externals of religion. Let us not despise each other for differing in lesser matters, but endeavour to promote true reformed Christianity,

enemy of kings and bishops, and in himself the very bond of rebels; who was born, through seventy years and eighty books, to disturb the peace of the kingdom, and twice to attempt the ruin of the church of England; in the endeavour of which mighty mischiefs he fell short. For which, thanks be to God." Biog. Brit., vol. ii. p. 18. Hallam, vol. iii. p. 197.

* See the supplementary account at the end of Bishop Patrick's Autobiography. Sharp's Life, vol. i. p. 143. Thoresby's Diary, vol. i. p. 400.

† Queen Mary had received from Spanheim, a treatise in favour of union between the church and dissenters, which she put into Tillotson's hands; he wrote to Spanheim expressing his approval of the treatise. Birch's Life of Tillotson, pp. 233, 234.

the simple, primitive, lovely religion of Christ, and not of this or that party. "Let us show ourselves men and manly Christians, not swayed by trifles and little things, as children by this or that dress, or mode, or form of our religion."* But the latitudinarianism of Howe was little relished in those days of savage controversy. Philip Henry had been earnestly desirous that the union of the churchmen and dissenters might now be accomplished. He had prayed constantly for it, he had used all endeavours, "as he had opportunity, that there might be some healing methods found out and agreed upon." But when he heard the cry of the clergy, that the Puritans should not be let in again to disturb the church, the good man despaired, for "he saw himself perfectly driven from them."

The Nonconformists had not been relieved many months from persecution, before a bitter quarrel sprung up among themselves. The fault was chiefly with the Independents, who attacked the Presbyterians with extraordinary fierceness, denouncing them as Arminians, underminers of the gospel, heretics. Dr. Daniel Williams they accused of Socinianism, and drove him, with Howe, Bates, and other excellent men, away from the Hall where the London dissenting ministers preached. Had a few concessions been made whilst this dreadful controversy was raging, most of the Presbyterians would have joined the church, but it was as Lord Halifax said, the church people would rather turn Papists than admit the Presbyterians among them. Thousands, says Thoresby, might have been gained to the church by a few concessions.† The Convocation was not allowed to sit again

---

* Life of Howe, pp. 373, 377, 379, 381, 382, 384.

† Bogue and Bennett, in their History of Dissenters, lay the largest share of the blame on the Independents, and some on the Baptists. With them agree Burnet, Palmer, and Rogers; from these authors I have drawn my conclusions.—See Bogue and Bennett's History, vol. i. pp. 402, 403, 405, 407, 418. Thoresby's Diary, vol i. p. 374. Burnet vol. iv. pp. 444, 445, Nonconformists' Memorial, vol. i. p. 415, vol ii. pp. 147, 641, 642. Life of Howe, pp. 389, 393, 395, 399 to 403.

until 1700 ; Archbishop Tillotson, and his successor Archbishop Tenison, with the moderate party, hoping that men would become in time more calm, but the hope was not realised. The seventeenth century passed away, and still the same angry passions raged. The Lower House of Convocation increased in factiousness, aimed at an independence of the State, and treated the bishops with insolence ; at length, in 1717, its violence provoked the government to prorogue it, and it has never again had a license to proceed to business.*

Even twenty years after the revolution, Sancroft's design of reconciling dissenters was attacked with undiminished fury by the famous Dr. Sacheverell. He was a man much like Dr. Samuel Parker, conceited, insolent, scurrilous, and ambitious, with a very small measure of religion, virtue, learning, or good sense.† On November 5th, 1709, being invited to preach in St. Paul's Cathedral, before the Lord Mayor, he considered it his duty *to blow a trumpet in Sion, and open the eyes of the*

---

* Almost all the speakers chosen by the Lower House were violent, factious men ; none of them, except Atterbury, were noted for great abilities. What can we think of men who chose for their prolocutor, a base, ungrateful man like Woodward, in preference to Beveridge, a pious, learned, and moderate high churchman ? What can we think of men who appointed Dr. Binks as their prolocutor, a man who had preached a sermon before them, in which he contrasted our Saviour's sufferings with those of King Charles I., *giving the preference to the king's ?* A member of the House of Commons called it a "blasphemous sermon;" Burnet says its expressions were indecent. Kennet's Hist. vol. iii. pp. 594, 799, 800, 842, 855. Burnet, vol. iv. p. 509—514; vol. v. pp. 66, 67, 69, 193, 297 ; vol. vi. pp. 52, 112. Hallam, vol. iii. pp. 174, 244, 247. Lathbury's Hist. of Convocation, pp. 278, 308, 332. Thoresby's Diary, vol. i. pp. 359, 408.

† The Bishop of Lichfield refused to ordain him a priest " because of his ignorance and rude behaviour." The Bishop of Oxford writing to the Bishop of Lichfield, says, " He is really proud, and thinks too well of himself, which I have often told him in plain terms, and with as much severity as I could, though to little purpose. I am sorry to see the follies of the boy grow up with the man. I cannot think he will now presume to offer himself to me, or any other bishop than your lordship, for priest's orders ; but if he do, I am sure I will not lay my hands upon him." Kennet's Hist. vol. iii. p. 747, note *a*.

deluded people* to the manner in which the church was being ruined by the Bishops, Whigs, Low Churchmen and Dissenters. He says, "A man must be very weak, or *something worse*, that thinks or pretends that dissenters are to be gained or won over by any other grants and indulgences than *giving up our whole Constitution*."† The attempt to draw in dissenters is "spiritual legerdemain, fallacious tricking, and double dealing." He calls union, comprehension, and moderation, "canting expressions, they mean nothing but getting money and preferment, by holding in with persons of all parties and characters, halting between a diversity of opinions, and reconciling God and Belial." He reviles Archbishop Grindal as "a false son of the church, a perfidious prelate," and denounces as a "false brother," him who should dare to "lay open all those sacred boundaries of the church, to let in all sectarists and schismatics, of whatsoever wild, romantic, or enthusiastic notions, so as to make the house of God not only a den of thieves, but a receptacle of legions of devils." Having poured forth a torrent of abuse in language sometimes too gross to be repeated, "upon the false brethren," who are plainly the bishops and other chief persons in church and state,‡ he thus proceeds to speak of the comprehension scheme :—"This was indeed the ready way to fill the house of God, but with what? With pagan beasts, instead of Christian sacrifices, with such unhallowed, loathsome, and detestable guests as would have driven out the Holy Spirit of God, with indignation. This pious design of making our house of prayer a den of thieves, of reforming our church into a chaos, is well known to have been attempted several times in this kingdom,

---

* See the dedication of his sermon on "The perils of false brethren," to Sir G. Garrard.
† Sermon on "The perils of false brethren," p. 42, in "The Trial of Dr. Sacheverell, printed for Jacob Tonson, 1710."
‡ See Sacheverell's Trial, pp. 36, 37, 41.

and lately within our memory, when all things seemed to favour it, but that good Providence, which so happily interposed, against the ruin of our church, and blasted the long projected scheme of the ecclesiastical Achitophels. A scheme so monstrous, so romantic, and absurd, that it is hard to say whether it had more of villany or folly in it, and which even the sectarists of all sorts (who will not be satisfied with anything less than sovereignty)* exploded and laughed at as ridiculous and impracticable. It was doubtless a wise way to exemplify our *brotherly love and charity for the souls of men*, to put both them and ourselves into a gulf of perdition, by throwing up the essentials of our faith, and the uniformity of our worship."† In reply to this "high nonsense," as Addison called it, Dr. William Wake, then Bishop of Lincoln, and afterwards Archbishop of Canterbury, explained and defended in the House of Lords, Sancroft's scheme, and the design of the divines appointed by King William to revise the Liturgy, of whom he spoke in these high and just terms:—They were a set of men than which this church was never, at any one time blessed with either wiser or better, since it was a church, . . . and a design that I am persuaded would have been for the interest and peace of our church and state had it been accomplished.‡ But the majority

* A similarly absurd statement is made by Roger North: "Almost anything of ceremony or form had been yielded to them, if it would have been accepted; but nothing less than episcopacy, root and branch, would content them; and upon that point they broke, and set up a separation." North's Examen, page 437.

† He then says, that as "these false brethren" failed in carrying the *Conventicle* into the *Church*, they are now resolved to bring the *Church* into the *Conventicle*. Having failed by *comprehension to pull down* the church, they seek by *moderation to blow her up*. *Comprehension is open violence, moderation is secret treachery.*—Sacheverell's Trial, p. 41.

‡ Speech of Dr. W. Wake, Bishop of Lincoln, in the House of Lords, on March 17th, 1710. Sacheverell's trial produced good, it was a great opportunity for the Whigs to defend the glorious Revolution, and caused Bishop Wake to give the only account we have of Sancroft's scheme for revising the Liturgy and admitting dissenters into the church. I find no mention made of this part of Sacheverell's sermon, by the managers on the part of the Commons, except a passing allusion by Mr. Thompson.

of the clergy were with Sacheverell, they rallied round him as the champion of the church, and replied with alacrity to his summons to *"put on the whole armour of God."** Forty thousand copies of his worthless sermon were sold : the Tories thought it deserved a bishopric, were in high glee, and inflamed the nation, with the cry " The church in danger ;"† the Whigs foolishly condemned it to be burnt. He was immediately after his trial, presented to a valuable living in Shropshire ;‡ his journey to take possession of it was a display of insolence on his part, and folly on the part of those who adored him. Thousands of men flocked out of the towns to meet him : to kiss his hand was an honour eagerly struggled for by the blind multitude : a glimpse of "the ever-blessed wig of the holy man" was an event to be remembered with gratitude. As Sacheverell's opinions were those of the clergy, it was useless to expect that they would take any measures either to revise the Liturgy or enlarge the church.§

Baxter and Howe and Philip Henry, and all that genera-

---

* See Sacheverell's Letter to the Vice-Chancellor of Oxford, speaking of himself as representing the University. The violence of the High Church party may be understood by their conduct towards White Kennet, who became a Whig. They represented him as Judas Iscariot, in a picture of the Last Supper, in Whitechapel church, placed over the altar by the Rector.—Nicholls's Literary Anecdotes, vol. i. pp. 140, 397. Noble's Biog. Hist. vol. iii. pp. 88, 110.

† Mr. Harley, afterwards Lord Oxford, was at dinner at his house in Herefordshire, when he received a packet from London telling him of Sacheverell's sermon ; he snapped his fingers and cried out with exultation, " The game is up, get the horses ready immediately !" and at once he set forth for London. Nicholls's Literary Anecdotes, vol. i. p. 68.

‡ Selattyn, near Oswestry.

§ Sacheverell's Trial. Burnet, vol. v. pp. 420, 422, 430, 435 ; vol. vi. pp. 9, 10 ; and Lord Dartmouth's note, p. 165. History of Shrewsbury, note. Letters of Eminent Men : Smith to Hearne, Feb. 8th, 1707 ; Hearne to Anstis, July 18th, 1714 ; and Hearne's Diary, p. 201. Thoresby's Correspondence, vol. ii. pp. 232, 248. Flying Post, July 20th, 1710. Post Boy, Mar. 24th, Dec. 15th, 1713. Burnet's and Talbot's Speeches at Sacheverell's Trial.

tion passed away, and their successors, satisfied with the Toleration Act, ceased to strive for union with the church.

The fever and excitement of the seventeenth century were succeeded by the lethargy of the eighteenth; the great controversies which had agitated church and state died away; in our stately English Temple there was silence, when men slumbered and slept, until the voice of John Wesley,—the grandson of one of the ministers ejected at the Restoration,—was heard, awaking the sleepers to spiritual activity.* Then, when men awoke, they felt the restraints of THE ACT OF UNIFORMITY.

THUS have three glorious opportunities of healing old disputes and enlarging the foundations of the national church,—the first at the accession of James I., the second at the Restoration, the third at the Revolution,—been neglected; they have passed away for ever; none such will occur again. Thus were Baxter, Howe, Philip Henry, Manton, Bates, Calamy, Jacomb, Flavel, Charnock, Newcomen, Spurstow, Allein, Matthew Poole, Samuel Clarke, Gouge, and a host of pious men driven out of the church of England. Thus did disastrous councils prevail, —the Liturgy was reviewed by men whose minds were exasperated by recent sufferings, and whose consciences were dull and hearts hard,—the church was narrowed when it should have been enlarged,—new shackles were imposed on men's minds instead of old ones being struck off,—the clergy of the foreign reformed churches were excluded from the pulpits of

---

* John Westley, or Wesley, (the son of the Puritan rector of Charmouth, in Dorsetshire,) was ejected by the Act of Uniformity, from Whitchurch, in the same county. His son was Samuel, the rector of Epworth, and father of the famous John Wesley. Athenæ Oxon, vol. iv. p. 503. Birch's Life of Tillotson, p. 307, note. Nonconformists' Memorial, vol. i. p. 478.

the Anglican church,—and it was vainly thought that the free people of England would worship God in a strictly uniform fashion. Thus were the attempts made by the wise and good to restore the Puritans, defeated by the prevalence of the same unhallowed temper which blinded men to the wickedness and folly of ejecting them. An injury has been inflicted upon the church, which no legislation can repair. Yet, though we can no longer hope to see the people of England restored to the communion of the established church, much may be done to enlarge and strengthen it. The provisions of the fatal Act of Uniformity should be carefully examined; and it is impossible to desire a more fitting time than the present, for discussing this subject. We live in those calmer times for which good men longed but never saw, when the vile passions of former days no longer rage. The subject will be brought before the country by Lord Ebury, who has laid upon the table of the House of Lords two bills; by one he proposes to remove the mischievous declaration* required from the clergy of assent and

---

* It may interest my readers, to compare the declarations which have been proposed as substitutes for the subscriptions, &c., at present required from the clergy. Through the courtesy of one of the peers, I have obtained a copy of Lord Nottingham's Bill (1689); the declaration proposed (as a substitute for present subscriptions, &c.,) is as follows: "I, A. B., do submit to the present constitution of the church of England. I acknowledge that the doctrine of it contains in it all things necessary to salvation, and I will conform myself to the worship and the government thereof as established by law, and I solemnly promise in the exercise of my ministry to preach and practice according thereunto." Tillotson proposed the following: "I, A. B., do submit to the doctrine, discipline, and worship of the church of England, as it shall be established by law, and promise to teach and practice accordingly." Birch's Life of Tillotson, p. 169. The declaration proposed by Bishop Wilkins or Sir Matthew Hale (1668), is as follows: "I, A. B., do hereby profess and declare, that I do approve the doctrines, worship, and government established in the church of England, as containing all things necessary to salvation; and that I will not endeavour by myself or any other, directly or indirectly, to bring in any doctrine contrary to that which is so established: and I do hereby promise, that I will continue in the communion of the church of England, and will not do anything to disturb the peace thereof." Lord Ebury's Speech in the House of Lords, May 8th, 1860, p. 10. Stillingfleet's Irenicum.

consent to the Prayer Book; by the other he aims at giving more elasticity to the services of the church. How far Lord Ebury may succeed in effecting those very desirable changes, depends much on the course adopted by the bishops. But whatever may be the issue, he will have this satisfaction, that he has expressed his own sympathy with those illustrious statesmen and divines who struggled, though unsuccessfully, against the schismatical, hard policy of the Restoration. It is no mean honour to be classed with the Southamptons, Hales, Tillotsons, and Stillingfleets, of those days; and there can be no nobler objects to strive after than the relief of men's consciences, and the vindication of the justice of this generation, by the substitution for the unrighteous act of a profligate age, of one bearing the name of our beloved Queen, than whom no monarch more virtuous ever reigned over the empire of Great Britain.

J. O. SANDFORD, PRINTER, HIGH STREET, SHREWSBURY.

THE FOLLOWING EDITIONS HAVE BEEN USED FOR REFERENCES:—

BAXTER'S Life and Times, 1696.
Basire's Correspondence, 1831.
Birch's Life of Tillotson, 1753.
Biographia Britannica, second edition.
Browne's (Sir Thos.) Works, 1836.
Burnet's History of his Own Time, 1823.
Calamy's Abridgment of Baxter, 1702.
Cart's Life of Ormond, 1736.
Carwithen's History of the Church of England, 1849.
Clarendon's State Papers, 1767-86.
Clarendon's Life, written by himself, 1761.
Clarendon's History of the Rebellion, 1826.
Collier's Ecclesiastical History, 1845.
Correspondence and Diary of Henry, Earl of Clarendon, 1828.
Echard's History of England, 1720.
Ellis's Original Letters, second series, 1827.
Evelyn's Memoirs and Diary, 1818.
Fox's History of James II., 1808.
Granger's Biographical History of England, 1779.
Guizot's History of Richard Cromwell and the Restoration, 1856.
Gutch's Collectanea Curiosa, 1781.
Hale (Sir Matthew) Life of, by Williams, 1835.
Hallam's Constitutional History of England, 1855.
Hallam's Literature of Europe, 1837-39.
Harleian Miscellany, 1793.
Heber's Life of Jeremy Taylor, prefixed to his works, 1828.
History of Dissenters, by Bogue and Bennet, 1808.
Howe's Life, by Henry Rogers, 1836.
Hutchinson's (Mrs.) Memoirs, 1806.
Kennet's History of England, 1719.
Lathbury's History of the Convocation, 1842.
Letters by Eminent Persons and Aubrey's Lives, 1813.

Life of Philip Henry, by Matthew Henry, 1765.
„   Dr. John Owen, prefixed to his works, 1850.
Lingard's History of England, 1823-31.
Locke's Life, by Lord King, 1829.
Macaulay's History of England, 1859.
Marsden's History of the Early Puritans, 1853.
„   „   Later Puritans, 1852.
Marvell's Works, 1776.
Milton's Prose Works, 1806.
Neal's History of the Puritans, 1793-1797.
Nicholls's Literary Anecdotes, 1812-15.
Noble's Continuation of Granger, 1806.
Nonconformists' Memorial, 1775.
North's Examen, 1740.
North's Lives of the Norths, 1826.
Oldmixon's History of England, 1730.
Patrick's Autobiography, 1839.
Pepys's Memoirs, 1825.
„   Life and Correspondence, 1841.
Ralph's History of England, 1744.
Rapin's History of England, 1733.
Rushworth's Collections, 1680-1701.
Sancroft's Life, by D'Oyly, 1821.
Secret History of Charles II., 1792.
Sharp's Life, by Newcome, 1825.
Somers Tracts, 1795.
Sparrow's Collection of Canons, 1684.
State Trials, 1776-81.
Thoresby's Diary, 1830.
Thoresby's Letters, 1832.
Warwick's Memoirs, 1813.
Waller's Life, 1727.
Welwood's Memoirs, 1718.
Wood's Athenæ Oxonienses, 1813-20.
Wordsworth's Ecclesiastical Biography, 1839.
Zurich Letters, Parker Society.

www.ingramcontent.com/pod-product-compliance
Lightning Source LLC
Chambersburg PA
CBHW030318170426
43202CB00009B/1058